PLANT BASED GUT HEALTH

A Simple 11-Step Guided Plan To Reset Your Microbiome, Lose Weight, & Prevent Your Allergy Triggers & Inflammation

This is really important.
It's a sincere thank you.

My name is Wayne, the founder of LearnWell.

My Dad put a book in my hands when I was 13. It was written by Zig Ziglar and it changed the course of my life. Since then, it's been books that have helped me get over breakups, learn how to be a good friend, study the lives of good people and books have been the source of my persistence through some pretty challenging times.

My purpose is now to return the favor. To create books that might be the turning point in the lives of people around the world, just like they've been for me. It's enough to almost bring me to tears to think of you holding this book, seeking information and wisdom from something that I've helped to create. I'm moved in a way that I can't fully explain.

We're a small and 'beyond-enthusiastic' team here at LearnWell. We're writers, editors, researchers, designers, formatters (oh ... and a bookkeeper!) who take your decision to learn with us incredibly seriously. We consider it a privilege to be part of your learning journey. Thank you for allowing us to join you.

If there's anything we did really well, anything we messed up, or anything AT ALL that we could do better, would you please write to us and tell us (like, right now!) We would love to hear from you!

readers@learnwellbooks.com

We're sending you our thanks, our love and our very best wishes.

Wayne

and the team at LearnWell Books.

LearnWell Books

At LearnWell, we think learning is the most important thing a person can do. Learners grow, lead, and solve important problems. We consider it a privilege that you've chosen one of our books to learn from.

In return, we have invested significant effort in creating what we believe are the best books in the world, on the topics we choose to write about.

Your book comes with several complementary features, including:

 ## WORKBOOK

Accompanying this book is a comprehensive Workbook that will enhance your learning and increase your knowledge retention.

Before reading, please get your copy of the Workbook here:

www.learnwellbooks.com/healthygut

It contains exercises that match the content of each chapter. It's interactive, user-friendly and proven to be the best way to absorb the valuable information in this book.

 ## EMAIL LEARNING COURSE

As we write our books, we conduct enormous amounts of research. Not all of what we discover ends up in the books but some of this information is highly relevant and deserves to be shared. So, our writers capture these interesting 'side-notes' in a series of short emails. These messages become like a private tutorial. Similar to having the writer sitting with you as you read, sharing their thoughts and insights.

If you choose to get the Workbook, you will also be entitled to receive this online tutorial, at no charge.

CO-AUTHOR

Our internal team of writers creates our books. We collaborate together, research together, edit each other's manuscripts, and collectively take responsibility for the written work we produce.

Sometimes we will seek input from a subject matter expert who can add meaningful insight on a topic. We interview that expert, often adopt their tone and style and refer to them in the first person. On this occasion, we worked with ...

Anita Tejani (MSc)

One of the pioneers of the concept of gut health as the basis for overall well being.

Anita is a nutritional scientist carrying a Master of Science in Personalised Nutrition and a Bachelor of Science focussed in Human Biology. Anita has worked with global leaders in health and sciences to uncover novel therapies and improve healthcare education. She has also worked directly with thousands of people worldwide to improve their health for the long-term.

To my gut microbiota,

100 trillion strong, a bustling
metropolis inside of me.

You work tirelessly, a microbial
community setting me free.

With wonder and appreciation
for the magic you perform, I owe
my health and vitality to this
extraordinary swarm.

CONTENTS

WORKBOOK

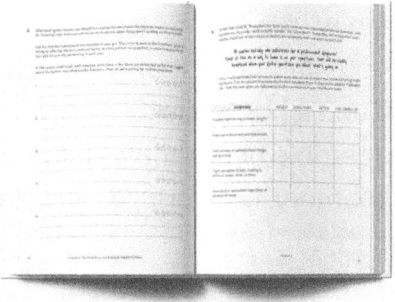

The average reader remembers just 14% of what they read. To dramatically enhance the amount of knowledge you absorb on this important topic, we have produced a user-friendly Workbook that follows the content of this book, chapter by chapter. Before beginning this book, make sure you receive a copy of your Workbook. Follow the link below:

Get Access To Your Free Workbook Here:

www.learnwellbooks.com/healthygut

INTRODUCTION

My entire life changed at the age of 22.

It was the summer of new beginnings. I had just graduated with my Bachelor's degree, got a job, and moved into a new apartment in downtown New York. I was so excited to get started and build something of my own. I was bursting with energy and an overwhelming desire to prove myself.

My symptoms began with a bit of fatigue. Concentrating on my work became difficult, and I constantly felt worn out. I woke up one morning and found a horrible skin rash. My digestive system went haywire, I had terrible headaches, and restful sleep at night became a distant memory. My work got affected, and I became an emotional mess.

My condition worsened from there as I developed food intolerance. It seemed everything I ate made me break out in hives and gave me painful stomach cramps. I would react to things like tomatoes and eggplant. My condition made me dread eating out with my friends or attending family dinners, and I confined myself to my apartment.

I could see my life crumbling around me. *I could not go on like this.*

It was time to fight for my health. I was willing to do whatever it took to get my life back. I visited the best doctors in my area, spent hours in hospital waiting rooms, and even traveled across the world to see specialists who I thought could "cure me." My efforts were all in vain. I got to hear the same thing over and over again: no conclusive diagnosis.

The disappointment and frustration I felt back then could not be put into words. My symptoms had brought my life to a standstill, yet there was nothing medical experts could do for me. My anger gave rise to defiance; I refused to accept that I simply had to endure chronic exhaustion, stomach cramps, frequent headaches, and severe sensitivity to foods for the rest of my life.

After visiting several doctors around the globe, I decided to take matters into my own hands and began doing my own research. I was enrolled in a Master of Science program in Personalized Nutrition. Studying subjects such as genetics and molecular biology helped me understand my problem better. My education shaped how I viewed my deteriorating health and helped take me out of a state of self-pity. Eventually, my distress gave way to curiosity. Nobody cared about my health as much as I did, and I was determined to find answers.

Today, I am living my best life because I decided not to give up on myself when everyone around me told me it was a lost cause. When my symptoms first appeared, I had no clue that it could all be because of one organ. Staying up late at night poring over books, perusing research papers and scanning medical files made me realize that all my problems boiled down to one thing: poor gut health.

My body was finding it hard to function because, all this time, my gut had been suffering. The news came as a bit of a shock; after all, I thought I was taking great care of my health. I didn't eat junk food (*a lot*), and I exercised (*occasionally*). The more I learned about the various factors that affect gut health, the more I realized everything I'd been doing wrong.

By writing this book, I intend to help people who are going through the same agony I found myself in all those years ago. Abdominal discomfort, bloating, indigestion, reflux, and insomnia can turn anyone's life upside down. Knowing why your body is acting up and what you can do to fix it makes you feel in control.

It took years of hard work and research for me to come up with an effective strategy to deal with my numerous issues. I've compiled all the knowledge I acquired during my journey to help you get a head start. Through this book, you'll understand precisely what's going on in your gut and realize that you're not a hostage to your strange symptoms. Good health is achievable, and you have everything it takes to turn your life around.

So, sit back and buckle up as we go on a ride into the fascinating world inside your gut.

Anita Tejani

Nutritional Scientist (MSc, BSc)
Subject Expert at LearnWell

PART 1

I Know I Should Feel Better Than This

1

Welcome! This is your first step towards a healthier gut ... and life!

COULD A HEALTHIER GUT BE THE ANSWER?

Good health is not something we can buy. However, it can be an extremely valuable savings account.

– Anne Wilson Schaef
American clinical psychologist and author

Imagine a baseball game. The crowd roars as the players stride onto the field and take their positions. The batter flexes his grip while the pitcher fixes his opponent with an intense gaze. In one swift motion, the pitcher sends the ball hurtling toward the batter, who swings with all his might, zipping the ball into the air. A wild frenzy erupts as the game unravels, and both teams scramble to beat the other. The batter dashes toward first base, the outfielders chase after the ball, and thunderous cheers echo through the stadium. The atmosphere is electric. The pressure mounts as the game inches to a close, and the players push themselves to their limits in a bid to win.

While the shiny, gold trophy is undoubtedly a great incentive, stripped bare of the glitz and glamor, the motivation to beat the other team comes down to a basic human instinct: *survival*. Ultimately, the team with the sharpest wit, strength, agility, and composure on the field clinches victory.

The teams dueling it out on the field are great crowd pullers. However, the survival instinct isn't limited to the stadium or humans alone. The urge to survive causes giant gray whales to swim thousands of miles to escape the frigid waters of the Arctic in winter. It sends small rodents scurrying into burrows, propels birds to soar in the sky to evade predators, and causes microscopic organisms such as bacteria to multiply at astonishingly fast rates.

As strange as it may sound, the riveting baseball game described above is, in essence, similar to the complex processes going on inside one of the most important organs in your body—your gut. Zooming in on this vital organ reveals a biological chain of events that resembles a fierce sports competition. Two teams of voracious single-celled microorganisms (tiny creatures that can only be observed under a microscope) go all out against each other, turning your gut into a battleground.

The tiny microbes battling it out against the backdrop of the mucosal lining of your gut can have a huge impact on your health. The effects may not be apparent right away, but gradually lead to myriad problems influencing your overall well-being. The conflict brewing inside your gut may seem inconsequential, but it can have an enormous effect on the quality of your life.

For years, I struggled with my health with no answers in sight. The lack of energy, insomnia, food intolerance and perpetual brain fog hampered my life. My numerous doctors' visits could not shed light on what was wrong.

Time and again, I was forced to simply accept my symptoms and learn to live with them. When I refused to do so, I was told I was wasting my time; I would keep running around in circles because the answer—whether I liked it or not—would stay the same: everything was all right.

My scientific background in genetics and microbiology made me question the explanations provided to me by specialists for so long. My subsequent investigation led me to Bali, Indonesia, which held a reputation as a healing destination. It was there I made a startling discovery.

I came across stories similar to my own as I interacted with the locals. Many people managed to heal themselves by changing their nutrition and lifestyle. This eye-opening experience convinced me to pursue my Masters of Science in Personalized Nutrition back home.

I researched the topic of nutrition in connection to my symptoms, using myself as the proverbial guinea pig, and the results were nothing short of astounding. Just as I suspected, even though everything appeared all right on the surface, the inside of my gut told an entirely different story. An epic showdown between two groups of bacteria was underway, and the bad news was my home team was losing. The more the visiting team piled on the runs, the more my symptoms flared up and the more discomfort I experienced.

The microbial tug-of-war going on inside me was taking its toll on my body. My only silver lining was that I could finally point to an organ and single it out as the source of all my troubles. *Here's where things are going wrong.* Now, the question was, how could I set them right? It took a few more years for me to fully understand the complicated biological processes and microbial interactions; however, I was able to change my life for the better once I made sense of the chaos.

Relief washed over me as I realized my situation was no longer hopeless. My research had put me in a position where I could devise the perfect strategy for my home team to shift the game's momentum and snatch victory from the jaws of defeat.

Perhaps the most shocking discovery I made was how I'd been unwittingly providing fuel to harmful microbes and starving the good ones all this time. I'd been cheering on the opposing team as they battered the home team!

Can you relate?

The knowledge I gathered helped me start taking small steps toward a healthier lifestyle. It became clear that I had to put myself first because nobody cared more about my health than I did. Changing my diet and lifestyle helped restore the balance between the warring bacteria inside my gut. Consequently, my energy levels went up, the mood swings stopped, and I started enjoying better health.

As I learned the hard way, keeping track of our gut health is crucial if we want to live a carefree, unproblematic, and active life. Today, I'm in a wonderful place in my life. I feel energetic, confident, and clear-headed. I'm so grateful that I can now eat all the foods I like without reacting to them. However, the journey to get here was not an easy one. My path was riddled with doubts, hardships, and disappointments.

Once I overcame my illness, I embarked on a mission to help others prevail over this awful condition. I created this book to guide people who may be going through the symptoms that made life unbearable for me at one point. The simple, step-by-step instructions in this book will help you take back the reins and rejuvenate yourself.

Change can be terrifying. The first step is always the hardest, but resigning yourself to pain and misery comes at a greater cost. As I experienced firsthand, poor health damages you in more ways than one: it chips away at your self-esteem, robs you of your ambition, snatches away your freedom, and forces you to give up on your dreams.

I'm here to remind you that you don't deserve to spend your life on the sidelines. You deserve to be on the field, in the middle of all the action, calling the shots. I want to make you feel empowered by showing you how to break free from everything that's holding you back.

GUT HEALTH: WHAT IT MEANS AND WHY IT MATTERS

The food you eat begins its long and eventful journey inside your body from the mouth. From here, it rolls into a long tube called the esophagus, which goes down to your stomach. Think of food as raw material shipped to a manufacturing company that churns out essential parts of a machine. The stomach breaks down food into small components that are processed further in the small and large intestine until they finally reach the assembling unit, where they're put together to produce goods that keep us feeling healthy.

The esophagus, stomach, and intestines work together and make up the gastrointestinal (GI) tract or the gut. Food is broken down in the gut into simpler forms that can enter the bloodstream, delivering nutrients throughout the body. For example, green, leafy vegetables and citrus fruits provide antioxidants and vitamins A, C, and E, which shows up in our hair, nails, and skin. Nuts and avocados are packed with unsaturated fats that protect our heart.

As long as the mechanism inside the GI tract works smoothly, our body receives a steady supply of essential nutrients that help it function to the best of its ability. And while it may seem like food and enzymes are the only occupants, our gut is teeming with microorganisms that help us digest the food we consume, but not all of them are our allies.

This is 'Gut Health'!

"Gut health" represents the function and balance of good and bad bacteria in the GI tract. When organs in the GI tract work together, we eat and digest food without discomfort. A healthy gut has a greater population of beneficial bacteria and immune cells to extract nutrients and fight off diseases. Digestive problems arise when something tips the balance, and the bad bacteria outnumber the good ones, making us susceptible to multiple illnesses.

Almost 62 million people suffer from digestive disorders each year in the U.S. alone (GI Alliance, 2021). The numbers are much higher worldwide, with a survey of 73,000 people from 33 countries suggesting that nearly 40% of adults suffer from gastrointestinal problems (Sperbe et al., 2021). Compelling evidence indicates that poor gut health can lead to severe digestive issues (Zhang et al., 2015). However, the symptoms are sometimes so subtle that they may go unnoticed for years.

WHAT YOUR GUT'S TRYING TO TELL YOU

Identifying poor gut health can be tricky, but some telltale signs can help you get to the root of the problem before it's too late. The discomfort we experience due to compromised gut health is our body's way of telling us something's not right. Here are five signs that the situation is getting out of control inside your gut.

1. **Weight Gain**

    Stepping on the scales and seeing the numbers go up can lead to a crushing sense of disappointment, especially when you've been trying your best to shed some pounds. Your mind instantly goes back to the last thing you ate, and you start counting calories. Embarrassment, shame, and resentment creep in as you remember the pizza you had yesterday or the fried chicken you munched on the day before.

If you're struggling to keep the weight off, don't be too hard on yourself because it could be a sign of an unhealthy gut.

2. **Skin Issues**

Skin problems such as acne, psoriasis, dermatitis, and rosacea can turn up in response to an imbalance in the gut. During the peak of my illness, painful skin rashes and hives started appearing on my skin. A glance at my reflection in the mirror would make my confidence take a sharp dive. It made me cut myself off from the world and lock myself in my room on my worst days. Socializing with others and even spending time with my family became a huge challenge.

Angry red pimples, itchy dry patches, or skin rashes can be frustrating to deal with and may shatter your self-esteem. If a trip to the dermatologist doesn't achieve much, it's probably best to focus inward.

3. **Bloating and Gas**

Harmful gut bacteria break down food and produce gas as a byproduct. Gas build-up can cause bloating and abdominal discomfort. Some unpleasant ways to relieve the pain associated with bloating include belching and flatulence, which can make social interactions extremely awkward.

4. **Sleep Problems**

Your mood is closely tied to how many hours of sleep you clock up at night. Without a good night's sleep, you're bound to wake up feeling irritable, moody, and downright cranky. Mental fatigue, exhaustion, and mood swings are common consequences of sleep deprivation.

If you're struggling to get some much-needed shut-eye at night, and you've ruled out every other reason, then the most likely culprit is poor gut health. You'll find it much harder to fall asleep with an unhealthy gut, and counting sheep won't help!

5. **Sugar Cravings**

Indulging your sweet tooth more often than you should often leads to guilt, anger, and a growing waistline, but there could be another reason why you find it hard to resist sugary treats.

The harmful bacteria in the gut thrive on sugar. These clever little microbes have devised a brilliant mechanism to make us consume more sugar by secreting proteins that mimic hunger-regulating hormones. As a result, we reach out for more sugary foods, packing on the pounds and making the bad guys stronger.

The symptoms above are only some ways your body calls for help. If you suffer from some or all of these conditions, then chances are you may have already tried finding solutions. I know just how aggravating it can be to put all your effort into finding a cure and come up empty.

Did you tick any of these 5 boxes?

The 11 steps outlined in the upcoming chapters encapsulate the knowledge I gained after years of meticulous research. Following these simple steps helped me get rid of the grueling symptoms of poor gut health, and they will help you achieve the same.

PLANT-BASED DIET: THE SECRET TO A HEALTHY LIFE

I know what it feels like to have no control over your life. The lack of energy, mood swings, indigestion, and insomnia had pushed me to the brink until I finally decided I'd had enough. But, what frustrated me more was how my initial attempts to recover were met with skepticism and disdain. Every doctor I visited told me the same thing: "You're all right." As for my debilitating symptoms, they told me to simply *learn to live with them*. No matter how much these specialists tried to convince me, I couldn't bring myself to accept this as my fate. I couldn't resign myself to a dull, miserable life marked by pain and suffering.

I kept telling myself: *"This can't be it,"* as I struggled to make it through each day due to chronic fatigue, stomach pains, and food intolerance. I didn't know back then that millions of people before me had been fed the same story and forced to live with their symptoms.

My goal with this book is to change how you look at food, so you can supplement the foods you love with nutrient-rich options. Armed with the information in this book, you'll be able to whip up a flavorsome, colorful meal that is not only a delight for your senses but packed with energy and nutrients.

Adopting a healthier lifestyle will increase your chances of living a long, fulfilled life, but it won't be a walk in the park. Replacing old habits with new ones will take a lot of work, but the bright side is that you can turn to this book for guidance to help you make it through the hard times.

I can tell you with full confidence that your present-day reality does not define you, and you have everything it takes to change your future. The stage is set, and the players are ready. Nothing can stop you once you know the ins and outs of the game. It's time to walk into the arena and fight to win.

 Go to your Workbook where you'll find helpful information related this chapter. If you haven't already, get your copy now at: www.learnwellbooks.com/healthygut

2

WHAT IS ACTUALLY GOING ON DOWN THERE?

The road to health is paved with good intestines!

—Dr. Sherry Rogers M.D.

A 6.7 magnitude earthquake rattled Los Angeles in 1994 at 4:30 a.m., causing a massive power cut that plunged the city into darkness. The trembling startled the sleeping residents, who rushed out of their homes or gazed through their windows to assess the damage inflicted on their neighborhoods. It was unnerving to see the city of lights shrouded in darkness; however, a glance at the sky above left them aghast.

The power outage had snuffed out the city's lights, unveiling the brilliant night sky. Lit up with a thousand glittering stars, the night sky was a magnificent sight. However, at that moment, the breathtaking beauty of the luminous sky caused a ripple of anxiety. Residents observed a strange silver cloud hovering above and, in a fit of panic, called 911.

The cloud that amazed the city dwellers turned out to be our galaxy, the Milky Way. With streetlights, neon signs, illuminated houses, buildings, and casinos blotting out the stars for decades, the dark sky sprinkled with a million specks of lights suspended in a white haze was an unusual sight for the urbanites.

Almost 100 to 400 billion stars shine in our Milky Way galaxy alone. With that number in mind, it's difficult to wrap your head around the massive size of the rest of the universe. The star-strewn sky instantly brings home the idea of the sheer vastness of the universe and the tiny space we occupy within it, smashing egos and helping us gain a unique perspective on our problems.

The plethora of cosmic bodies that adorn the obsidian sky at night evoke a slew of emotions, ranging from fear to wonder. But perhaps even more astonishing is the microbial cosmos enclosed within the human body that is no less complex, remarkable, and spellbinding than the splendid night sky.

100 trillion microorganisms occupy your gut, exceeding the number of human cells in your body. An entire universe of bacteria, fungi, and viruses is tucked inside us. Your gut resembles a bustling city center on a Monday morning, with the traffic tied up for miles and overcrowded sidewalks. While we may not be aware of the microcosm locked inside us, its impact on our lives is undeniable.

WAIT! DID YOU SAY 100 TRILLION?

It's a mind-bending concept that transformed the world of medicine when it was uncovered. To understand how this discovery came about, let's pack our bags and travel back in time to 17th-century Netherlands.

We find ourselves in the idyllic countryside, with the sun shining down on us and rolling green plains stretching as far as the eye can see. The shimmering water of a pond catches our attention, and we glimpse a middle-aged gentleman in unusual attire standing at its edge. His old-fashioned clothes give us an idea that the year is 1665, and we quietly watch him bend down on one knee and fill a glass jar with water.

The gentleman we just saw is the Dutch merchant, Antonie Van Leeuwenhoek (lay-vuhn-huk), who is about to stroll back to his house and observe a drop of the water he collected under his microscope. Pressing his eye against the lens, Leeuwenhoek sees green streaks of algae and several small creatures darting back and forth across his field of vision. He names them "Animalcules," meaning tiny animals.

Previously, driven by his curiosity, Leeuwenhoek developed powerful microscopes with sophisticated lenses that opened a window into an invisible world unknown to others. He became obsessed with his new gadget, much like how we get hooked to new technology in modern times, and collected thousands of samples from his environment and himself to observe under the microscope. His passionate explorations made him the first person to set sights on the diverse and abundant life forms that colonize virtually every nook and cranny of our planet.

In 1681, he noted the presence of thousands of microorganisms in a sample of his stools. A sample of dental plaque taken from his own teeth two years later also revealed a multitude of microbes. Leeuwenhoek's findings suggested a flush of microorganisms colonized the human body, but it wasn't until the 19th century rolled in that scientists got their first glimpse of gastrointestinal bacteria.

Let's continue our time-traveling adventures, this time to the year 1842. We find ourselves in a cluttered room in Edinburgh, England, where we see a grim-faced surgeon named John Goodsir shuffling toward the microscope on his desk with a slide in his hand. He sits on a chair that creaks loudly in protest, fits the slide on the stage, and peers through the lens, adjusting one of the knobs to get a better look.

The sample mounted on the slide was taken this morning from the vomit of his 19-year-old patient. The boy had been suffering from a dreadful illness that made him throw up a watery fluid every day without fail. The surgeon was taken aback by what he saw—the sample was brimming with bacteria that looked like a small bundle of cells tied with string!

Looking back from the 21st century, we can see that John Goodsir's discovery was a giant leap for medicine that opened new avenues for treating diseases. Goodsir named the microorganism he saw in his patient's vomit *Sarcina ventriculi*, declaring it the causative agent of his patient's sickness. In view of his findings, his patient was medicated with creosote drops, an antiseptic (a substance that prevents the growth of microorganisms), which helped him recover.

Over the years, our understanding of microorganisms has evolved in light of new research, ever since the first bacteria were observed under a microscope. By the time the curtain closed on the 19th century, the presence of microorganisms in the human body had been firmly established. Today, we know that the largest number of microorganisms are found in the human gut and that they can exist peacefully in a healthy person (Harvard T.H. Chan School of Public Health, n.d.).

GUT MICROBIOME: THE INVISIBLE ORGAN

Let's revisit the busy city center: the din of traffic, vehicles crawling along the road, and pedestrians flooding the sidewalks. If you look closely, you can make sense of the confusion and see patterns emerge from the chaos.

Every single person caught in the morning rush is essential for the city: the bankers, the doctors, the cab drivers, and the couriers. To keep everything running smoothly, it is important for each group of people to continue performing their duties. A single institution going on a strike is enough to bring the city grinding to a halt.

Like the city above, the gut microbiome is a collection of diverse microorganisms living in the GI tract. It is responsible for so many important functions that some scientists go as far as calling it a "supporting organ." The microbiome inside the human body helps maintain a healthy environment; however, diet, stress, and inflammation can disrupt its function.

Every person has a unique selection of microorganisms colonizing their body, determined by their DNA. We are first exposed to microbes when we're born. Our first brush with microorganisms happens in our mother's birth canal during delivery and through nursing. So, the network of microbes we're exposed to during our early years depends largely on our mother's microbiome. However, our environment and diet eventually take on a more prominent role in introducing new bacteria, viruses, and fungi. So, the microbiome we acquire as infants changes as we grow.

For example, studies have shown that at the age of 65 and above, the microbiome of physically active individuals differs from those who are less healthy and fit. Most notably, a 2020 review published in the journal *Nutrients* discovered a strong link between the gut microbiome and longevity (Badal et al., 2020). Greater microbial diversity also seems to contribute to physical robustness in old age. Moreover, microbiome of people belonging to different age groups varies greatly. Analyzing the microbiomes of people from diverse age groups showed a fascinating pattern of microbial diversity during an individual's life span.

For the first three years of life, the microbiome changes rapidly. It remains stable for the next several decades, undergoing changes during midlife. In old age, changes in the microbiome accelerate in healthy individuals but slow down and eventually become static in people who may be less healthy (O'Connor, 2021).

An interesting fact about the GI tract is that it's considered to be outside the human body because it's exposed (through the mouth and anus) to external factors. Its contents don't make contact with the other organs or filter into body cavities. The cheeseburger you ate for lunch does not seep into the bloodstream until completely digested. The absorption of nutrients and vitamins needed to keep our bodies functioning occurs in the small and large intestines. This explains how the GI tract keeps microorganisms trapped in the gut.

The bacteria that make up our microbiome can either be beneficial or harmful. Usually, the number of beneficial microbes (our home team) exceeds that of harmful microbes (the visiting team). However, in some cases, the balance shifts in favor of the visiting team, and all hell breaks loose. That's certainly what happened to me!

The opponents romped over my home team, leaving me battered and bruised. My gut health declined, and I was left writhing in pain. However, even at my lowest point, I decided to push through the pain and not give up. My research did not just help me understand my condition; it also introduced me to a new perspective on what makes us human.

BREAKING BARRIERS: THE HUMAN MICROBIOME PROJECT

We are all made up of cells containing genetic code or DNA, which is a set of instructions determining our looks, personality, proclivities, skills, and even the diseases we might suffer from as we age. Think of DNA as a colossal library crammed with mahogany shelves stacked with books. Each book represents a gene with a specific code written inside that only an experienced code breaker can decipher.

Microorganisms are also governed by genetic material, and since there are ten times more bacterial cells in our body than human cells, microbial genes significantly outnumber human genes (Turnbaugh et al., 2007). So, even though the size of microbial cells is only one-tenth to one-hundredth the size of human cells, they add at least five pounds to our body weight (Baylor College of Medicine, n.d.).

Our bodies may be overflowing with bacteria, but we still know very little about these tiny inhabitants. How much does the microbial population vary from person to person? How diverse are the bacteria that occupy a single individual? And what role they play in causing various diseases remains shrouded in mystery. Imagine walking into a library with shelves towering up to the ceiling and groaning under the weight of thousands of books, only you have no idea what's written inside.

Human and bacterial DNA became a tantalizing enigma for scientists determined to unravel the mysteries of the universe. Researchers first set out to decode human DNA in 1990 by launching an ambitious program called the Human Genome

Project (HGP). The HGP aimed to create a map of the human genome. The project concluded in 2003 and revealed 20,500 genes in the human genome. This was a massive blow for some scientists, who predicted the number to be close to 100,000. The idea that the number of protein-coding genes in humans was the same as that in a fruit fly was rather humbling.

Soon after, scientists decided to reimagine what constituted "human," extending their research to include the genes of the microorganisms living inside and on us and initiating the Human Microbiome Project (HMP) in 2007. Exploration of microbial DNA showed that microbes performed several vital functions humans cannot carry out independently.

Looking at the human body is the same as looking at a photo mosaic. Stepping closer to the frame brings into focus the tiny images that combine to make the bigger picture. But what's truly remarkable is how these individual photos bear little resemblance to the mammoth scene that caught our attention from afar. Likewise, some parts that humans are made of are not human at all, but those belonging to the tiny creatures colonizing our bodies—microbes.

Through the HMP, scientists hoped to gather enough data to help them understand the microbiome's role in health and disease. The HMP published its results in 2012 in the journal *Nature* (The Human Microbiome Project Consortium, 2012). The information gathered from this extensive study shed light on the incredible diversity of the microbiome and how it varied from one person to the other.

Just like fingerprints, the human microbiome is unique for each individual. However, despite crucial differences in the number and types of microorganisms, different microbial species perform similar tasks in different people. Another key finding in the HMP publication was how microbial communities clearly preferred certain locations in the human body. For example, the microbes on the skin vary from the ones found in the mouth or the intestines. The project also identified a few "signature" bacteria with genes that linked them to particular sites.

The HMP opened the world of medicine to exciting new ideas for treating disease. Since different microorganisms were camping out in various areas of the body, scientists wondered if they could prod these tiny creatures to perform their jobs more effectively. What if we could manipulate the bacteria in the gut to help us lose weight or heal from gastrointestinal disorders? The possibilities were endless!

WHAT MAKES GUT MICROBES IMPORTANT FOR US

The Human Microbiome Project altered our perception of health and disease and the role of microorganisms in the two. The gut microbiome is essential to human life, performing various critical functions. Some aspects of human health affected by gut bacteria include:

Nutrition

Let's imagine a slice of pizza covered with cheese, pepperoni, capsicum, and mushrooms. You get transported to heaven the moment you take the first bite, and the burst of flavor hits your taste buds. The taste, color, texture, and smell of food make eating a divine experience, but—to our eternal disappointment—it's not what our body needs to help it function. The second you swallow that bite, enzymes, and microbes inside the gut spring into action to extract energy and nutrients.

Gut microbes help your body absorb energy from that bite of pizza. They break down the complex compounds in meats, helping you wring out proteins from the pepperoni. They help digest plant cellulose, ripping apart the capsicum and digging up vitamins and minerals. And most importantly, they stop you from going for another slice by influencing food cravings and making you feel full.

Immunity

The mother's womb provides a safe, controlled environment. Cloistered inside the uterus, the baby's needs are met, and there's no room for unpleasant surprises. This period of relative peace and comfort is broken at birth. The fetus is squeezed through the narrow space of the cervix, making birth a rather traumatic experience and a rude awakening for the infant.

As infants, our first brush with microbes happens in the birth canal, as the microbes living there decide to hop on for a ride. These early microbial guests help us develop "Adaptive Immunity." The immune system is like a security checkpoint where every incoming person is frisked, their paperwork checked, and their luggage scanned.

The immune cells act like border patrol officers by preventing the entry of foreign objects inside the body. If someone does manage to slip in, the officers are quick to apprehend and toss them out and add their information to a criminal database. Remembering past criminals helps the officers fight them off in the future; this is known as "Adaptive Immunity."

The onslaught of microorganisms in the birth canal expands the immune system's criminal database, protecting us from a wide range of diseases and infections later on in life. In contrast, rodents prevented from exposure to microorganisms in a laboratory setting developed a weaker immune system, making them susceptible to a number of health problems later on.

Behavior

The gut microbiome is not only involved in carrying out different functions in the body of its own accord; it also plays a crucial role in affecting our thoughts. Some scientists even label the microorganisms inhabiting our gut a "second brain." Gut microbes pulling the strings of your brain is a freaky concept, but there's plenty of evidence to back it up.

The activity of gut bacteria releases chemical molecules that trigger nerves in the GI tract. The bridge between the gut and the nervous system is called the "Gut-Brain Axis." Researchers have found strong ties between the microorganisms in the gut and psychological disorders such as depression and developmental problems such as autistic spectrum disorder (Clapp et al., 2017). I will discuss this in more detail in the upcoming chapters.

Disease

Disrupting the delicate balance between healthy and damaging bacteria can wreak havoc on our health, opening doors to several diseases such as inflammatory bowel disease (IBD), Crohn's disease, and ulcerative colitis. In addition, it affects energy levels, cognitive functions, and brain development, making everyday tasks a vast challenge—some of these symptoms might be unfortunately familiar to you. Overpopulation of harmful bacteria can also cause metabolic syndrome, a collection of conditions such as high blood pressure, elevated cholesterol levels, and high blood sugar that increase the likelihood of heart disease and stroke. Furthermore, individuals with low gut microbiome diversity are prone to obesity, IBD, and type 2 diabetes.

THE ROAD TO GOOD HEALTH

Sauerkraut, kefir, yogurt, kimchi, and kombucha—what do these foods have in common other than adding a punch of flavor to your meal? They're bursting with microorganisms. A 2021 study crowned these fermented foods as the champions of microbial diversity in the gut, crediting them for altering microbiome composition positively and reducing inflammation (Wastyk et al., 2021).

The "immune boosting" effects of a diet based on fermented foods and plant-based fibers have been proven by countless studies over the past decade. Moreover, in view of new research, scientists are also beginning to realize the significance of fungi in the gut microbiome in addition to bacteria. Unlike bacteria, fungi can be single-celled or multicellular organisms. These incredibly diverse creatures range from wild mushrooms growing in your backyard to microscopic organisms present in your gut.

Several key studies have pushed fungi into the spotlight, urging researchers to investigate their role in digestive diseases such as IBD. Research published in the journal *Science* found that *Debaryomyces hansenii* (a commonly used fungus in the food industry for surface ripening of meat and cheese) accumulated in inflamed tissues in patients with Crohn's disease. In laboratory mice, the rogue fungus was found to prevent wound healing by triggering the release of a chemical called CCL5 that inhibits the body from repairing the damage. Coincidentally, this is the same chemical responsible for IBD. The findings established a close connection between a specific group of microbes in the gut and intestinal inflammation, something that scientists had suspected all along (Jain et al., 2021).

I was thrilled when I found out that through certain diets, I could reduce inflammation and restore balance among different microbial populations in the gut. However, I soon learned that munching on more greens was not the only solution. Sometimes the gut microbes that make up our home team need backup. Probiotics such as *Lactobacillus* and *Bifidobacterium* are microorganisms that join forces with our home team to hammer the opposing team.

Introducing certain bacteria to the gut that could manipulate the microbiome is a concept that has existed for many years. However, new clinical trials showing the efficacy of using microbes to overcome hospital-associated diarrhea caused by *Clostridium difficile* (*Ferring Global*, 2021) streamlined support for this theory.

The cornucopia of microbes in the GI tract performs numerous functions. The gut microbiome's significant role in digestion, behavior, and immunity earned it the name of the invisible organ. The previously mentioned HMP further solidified the microbiome's significance in human health, shifting the medical community's focus on improving gut health.

Health problems impair everyday functions, causing considerable distress. We may consider our situation hopeless when we're getting hammered by a number of illnesses, but research shows us that there's a lot that we can do to regain strength and trounce our opponents.

PART 2

OK, Here's The Problem

3

IT'S BECAUSE
OF DYSBIOSIS
(DIS-BY-OH-SIS)

Health is the natural condition. When sickness occurs, it is a sign that Nature has gone off course because of a physical or mental imbalance. The road to health for everyone is through moderation, harmony, and a 'sound mind in a sound body'.

— Jostein Gaarder

During my visit to Bali, a black and white checkered cloth caught my eye. I saw it wrapped around people's waists, draped over stone statues, fastened to tree trunks and bedecking temples. Intrigued by the cloth's ubiquitous presence on the island, I set out to investigate its meaning.

I soon learned that the black and white textile signified Rwa Bhineda: the Balinese philosophy of balance and harmony. Similar to the Chinese belief of yin and yang, the black and white squares on the fabric represented mutual dualism. The cloth was called kain poleng and depicted an equal number of black and white squares, symbolizing the coexistence of opposites.

The kain poleng is a constant reminder of the importance of keeping balance and is often found tied around sacred objects to signify that a spirit resides within them. The Balinese people also believe the cloth grants protection against negative forces, so it is frequently found in places or wrapped around objects believed to emit negative energy. I was fascinated by the concept of Rwa Bhineda and how duality was central to so many cultures and religions.

The dark, cold night changes into a bright, sunny day. The stifling heat of the summer months is quelled by rain. Without sorrow, it's impossible to value joy, and the sweetest victories are always preceded by a long hard struggle full of pain and suffering. Ancient sages observed these polarities and concluded that happiness, health, and prosperity could only be achieved by striking the right balance between two opposing forces.

Just like the universe at large, the organs in the human body work together in harmony. Good health is contingent on achieving a delicate balance between different biological factors. The right amount of water, food, and nutrients are necessary to bring energy levels up, while adequate levels of enzymes, hormones, and chemicals ensure our bodies function like a well-oiled machine. Balance is key for good health, and stress, sleep, diet, and exercise are all factors that can easily tip the scales if they're not managed properly.

Balance is crucial for the gut microbiome as well. A truce between the warring microorganisms helps the gut microbiome function at its best, while conflict impairs its ability to carry out the tasks essential for good health. When the microbial community exists in peace and harmony, the gut microbiome performs its functions efficiently, boosting health and vitality.

THE MICROBES IN YOUR GUT AND WHAT THEY DO FOR YOU

A robust gut microbiome accounts for a number of biological functions and plays a critical role in maintaining health. We briefly discussed some of these in the previous chapter. However, you might be wondering exactly *how* they do it.

Let's find out what keeps them busy.

They Keep The Bad Guys Out

The small and large intestines are lined with a layer of epithelium cells responsible for restricting the entry of harmful substances and the absorption of nutrients. It functions the same way as a sieve used to sift flour; however, some "bad guys" can gnaw their way in and stir up trouble. Gut microbes make sure that doesn't happen by maintaining epithelial cell integrity. Like a bouncer at a nightclub, they kick out the intruders, preventing disease-causing bacteria from gaining access to the gut.

They Keep Things Moving

The muscles of the GI tract contract and relax in a wave-like motion, pushing the food down. This movement of the gut is called peristalsis, which maintains a constant flow of digestive contents such as microorganisms, food particles, and enzymes (chemicals that break down the food). The flow of the digestive contents through the GI tract prevents bacterial overgrowth.

The harmful bacteria can affect gut peristalsis by releasing excessive amounts of toxins that hinder fat absorption. This weakens the epithelial lining of the gut, affecting peristalsis. The disruption of gut motility causes unwanted bacteria to pile up where they shouldn't, leading to more problems. Imagine someone abruptly hitting the brakes in traffic and causing all the vehicles behind them to smash into each other (Waclawiková et al., 2022).

They Make Sure We Have Everything We Need

The microbiome runs a five-star restaurant in your gut, producing vitamins such as thiamine, folate, biotin, riboflavin, pantothenic acid, vitamin K, and folate (Morowitz et al., 2011). Moreover, bacteria in the colon break down leftover food particles that weren't absorbed into the bloodstream. These are transformed into short-chain fatty acids (SCFAs), which can easily pass through the epithelial membrane. SCFAs carry out a number of important functions in our bodies. We'll discuss these in detail in the next chapters.

If our home team gets trampled by its opponents, the bad guys can run the entire setup into the ground. Unabsorbed fats will start piling up, depleting our body of essential vitamins such as vitamin K, D, E, and A. Meanwhile, the build-up of gasses such as methane, hydrogen, and carbon dioxide begins causing abdominal discomfort, bloating, and flatulence (Doucleff, 2014).

They Keep The Engine Running

The friendly microorganisms in our gut keep our metabolism running, making sure our energy levels are full by breaking down complex foods and maintaining a steady supply of vitamins and minerals. A 2010 research published in *Diabetes Care* revealed the gut microbes' important role in maintaining healthy body weight and preventing Type 2 Diabetes (Musso et al., 2010). The introduction of beneficial microbes improved insulin sensitivity and helped the subjects shed weight, indicating the ability of these microorganisms to keep the metabolic machinery whizzing and whirring.

They Help Us Feel Better

Who can resist a big tub of ice cream or a box of chocolates, especially when we're feeling down. However, we don't realize that while we're gobbling up spoonfuls of chocolate ice cream, gut microbes are busy fixing our mood. The microbes in your gut produce a whopping 95% of serotonin, a neurotransmitter responsible for mood regulation, cognition, learning, memory, and generating feelings of reward.

The impact of this on your mental health is significant.

A neurotransmitter is a chemical messenger that transmits messages from neurons (brain cells) to target cells (muscles, glands, or other neurons). The neurons in our brain are separated by each other; the space between them is called a synapse. Messages in the brain travel as electrical impulses which can't travel through the empty space between neurons without the help of neurotransmitters. The electrical impulses hitch a ride with different neurotransmitters to reach the other side, activating a particular brain pathway.

Neurotransmitters behave the same way as an electric wire. They transmit electricity to the bulb at the end, lighting it up. However, if the wire snaps, the connection breaks—the bulb flickers and goes off. Dopamine, serotonin, and GABA are some neurotransmitters crucial for mood regulation and can be termed the "happiness molecules." The microbiome produces the happiness molecules that drive out stress and improve mental well-being by warding off depression and anxiety (Singh et al., 2021).

WHAT HAPPENS WHEN THINGS GO WRONG

So what's at stake if our home team gets thrashed by the visiting team? For starters, it upends a carefully crafted system designed to keep us in good shape. The effects of this upheaval ripple through the entire body, opening a can of worms.

Dysbiosis

Dysbiosis is "a reduction in microbial diversity and a combination of the loss of beneficial bacteria" (Blijlevens & van der Velden, 2020). Imagine a high-rise catching fire. As the flames mushroom, thick black smoke fills the rooms, replacing oxygen molecules and making breathing impossible. The raging fire eats away the building's framework, causing it to collapse in flames and leaving behind a smoldering mountain of debris.

If the building is well-equipped, the rising smoke will set off the smoke alarm, giving the residents enough time to evacuate and call the fire department. Think of dysbiosis as rising smoke particles that set off our body's alarm system. The symptoms of dysbiosis are the same as the sharp, screeching sound of the smoke alarm telling us to grab the fire extinguisher and put out the fire.

Symptoms Of Dysbiosis

- *Bad breath:* Small intestinal bacterial overgrowth (SIBO) and *Helicobacter pylori* lead to the breakdown of sulfur, releasing a rotten smell, which tends to come out through the mouth (New Life Nutrition, n.d.).

- *Digestive problems:* Chaos in the digestive system can cause an upset stomach, nausea, bloating, constipation and diarrhea. We will discuss this further in Chapter 9.

- Redness and skin rashes: Leaky gut resulting from the overgrowth of harmful microbes can cause the skin to become inflamed, leading to problems such as eczema and acne (*How Skin Relates to Gut Health*, n.d.).

- Cardiovascular problems: Unhealthy gut bacteria cause an increase in the amount of trimethylamine-N-oxide (TMAO), an inflammatory marker, elevated levels of which are linked to deteriorating cardiovascular health. We will discuss TMAO in more detail in chapter 11.

- Nutrient deprivation: We learned in the previous chapters that certain gut microbes help break down food, releasing nutrients and vitamins. The absence of these helpful microbes may lead to nutritional deficiencies.

- Frequent mood swings: As we learned in the previous section, the absence of beneficial bacteria maintaining a steady supply of neurotransmitters such as serotonin and dopamine can lead to depression, anxiety, or frequent bouts of fatigue.

- Weight gain: A growing number of sugar-loving bacteria and a lack of mood-regulating neurotransmitters make it harder to resist sugary and high-carb foods. We will learn more about the relationship between gut microbes and weight gain in chapter 7.

Identifying our symptoms and getting to the root of our problems can seem incredibly complicated sometimes. If you're finding it difficult to decide whether you suffer from dysbiosis or not, ask yourself these questions:

1. Are you having trouble maintaining a steady weight?

2. Do you often find yourself feeling sad without any concrete reason?

3. Do you feel anxious or worried about things going wrong almost every day?

4. Do you often feel a tight sensation in your belly that makes it difficult for you to eat, drink or even move?

5. Do you feel tired or exhausted no matter how much sleep you get?

If you answered yes to the above questions, you're checking off some boxes related to dysbiosis, and you should contact your healthcare professional.

What Sets Off The Alarm

After suffering from countless health problems for so many years, I felt a sudden pang of guilt when I found that dysbiosis was the reason for my poor health. *I had done this to myself.* My poor choices had landed me in so much pain. I felt I had no one to blame but myself, and it shattered my resolve to get better. I was determined to understand my situation as best as possible, so I continued my research. Factors such as antibiotic use, radiation treatment, stress, changes in gut peristalsis, and diet could crush the beneficial microbes in our gut, causing dysbiosis and its many terrible symptoms.

Antibiotics

Antibiotics are essential to help us beat a cold or sore throat and get back on our feet. While they are extremely effective in getting rid of several illnesses, frequent use of broad-spectrum antibiotics flattens beneficial microbial populations in the gut. Harmful microbial populations surge with the good bacteria no longer there to keep the bad guys in check. One such bacteria that spreads rapidly when the good bacteria start dying off is *Clostridium difficile*, which causes diarrhea.

We discussed above how a balanced gut microbiome produces short chain fatty acids (SCFAs), which play a vital role in water and electrolyte absorption in the colon. In addition, these nifty little molecules carry out several crucial functions such as improving blood flow, rapid calcium absorption, maintaining mucosal integrity of the colon, and increasing the absorptive ability of the small intestine. When the bad bacteria take over, the level SCFAs in the gut declines, and their many benefits are lost. With our trusted gatekeepers gone, it also becomes easier for the bad guys to sneak in and colonize the gut.

Stress

It's impossible to banish stress from our lives completely, but exposing ourselves to prolonged periods of psychological or physical stress can be detrimental to our health. Researchers set out to find the effect of stress on the gut microbiome following maternal separation in infant rhesus macaques. Within a few days of being separated from their mothers, the macaques showed declining populations of good bacteria (*Lactobacilli* and *Bifidobacteria*) in the gut, indicating changes in the internal environment.

Psychological stress was found to be associated with decreased mucin production and falling levels of acidic mucopolysaccharides. These are vital for providing lubrication for food passage, aiding communication between cells, and protecting from invading microbes. Rolling back production of these crucial substances in response to stress causes a significant increase in harmful microbial populations, upsetting the balance in a healthy gut microbiome.

In addition, stress suppresses the production of immunoglobulin IgA, weakening the immune system. This is akin to an army losing its most experienced and skilled General. Without the proper leadership, any attack on the enemy is bound to fail. A frail security system means we fall sick more often. Long periods of physical and mental strain also lead to rising levels of norepinephrine, which leads to burgeoning populations of disease-causing microbes.

Diet

A study published by Jason A. Hawrelak in 2004 shows that a diet rich in sulfur compounds increases the number of harmful bacteria in our gut, unleashing chaos in the gut microbiome. Foods laden with preservatives, dried fruits, shellfish, dehydrated vegetables, packaged fruit juices, white bread, baked goods, and most alcoholic beverages are sources of sulfur.

Consumption of foods rich in sulfur-containing amino acids such as meat, eggs, cow's milk, and cheese can also cause increased sulfide concentrations in the colon. A high-protein diet based on eggs and meat results in elevated levels of ammonia, which can hamper metabolism, alter gut morphology, and decrease the lifespan of mucosal cells. A protein-rich diet produces harmful chemicals such as indoles, amines, sulfides, and phenols, which are linked to several health problems such as migraines and schizophrenia and are thought to be cancer-causing (Hawrelak, 2004).

Diets high in sugars slow down the rate at which food moves along the GI tract, increasing bile production. Since many bacterial species thrive on bile acids, this may lead to a microbial imbalance in the gut, causing harmful bacteria to rise. Consuming large quantities of sugary foods also results in higher levels of inflammation and increased mucosal permeability (Hawrelak, 2004). This is essentially the same as leaving the gates wide open for the bad guys, so they can stroll inside and wage war on our bodies.

If we ever find ourselves lost somewhere, it helps to remember which way we came in. If you still have no clue about what could have upset the delicate balance in your gut microbiome, then go to exercise 2 of Chapter 3 in the Workbook. This exercise is specifically designed to help you figure out what could have incurred the wrath of the bacteria in your gut.

WHAT LIES IN STORE FOR US

Before we can load you up with tips and tricks, we need to get familiar with what exactly is at stake. So, let's gaze into our crystal ball and see what lies in store for patients suffering from dysbiosis.

An imbalance in the gut microbiome opens a Pandora's box of health problems that can make life quite miserable. These include diseases associated with the digestive system, metabolic disorders such as obesity and type 2 diabetes, and disorders of the central nervous system that affect mood and behavior. Major health disorders resulting from dysbiosis include:

- Inflammatory bowel disease (IBD)

- Type 2 diabetes

- Ankylosing spondylitis

- Atopic eczema

- Rheumatoid arthritis

- Irritable bowel syndrome (IBS)

- Obesity

- Metabolic syndrome

This paints a rather frightening picture of what the future holds for people living with dysbiosis. The good news is that you're in the driving seat. So, even if it seems you're speeding toward disaster, you can slam the brakes and take a different route. The following chapters will help you develop a roadmap to break free from dysbiosis and live your best life.

HOW IT IMPACTS
THE REST OF
YOUR BODY

*Good nutrition and vitamins do not directly cure disease;
the body does. You provide the raw materials, and the
inborn wisdom of your body makes the repairs.*

—Andrew Saul

The clip-clop of a horse's hooves pierces through the deathly silence in the abandoned old western town. The sun blazes down on the weather-beaten buildings lining the dirt road. A gust of wind kicks up a thick cloud of dust and a ball of tumbleweed rolls past. A lone ranger riding a horse appears when the dust settles. He squints at the false front buildings, his jaw clenched, and his sharp, beady eyes scan every inch of the landscape. Clad in cowboy boots and hat, the rugged hero hunting down outlaws and keeping the peace is our most trusted warrior: the short-chain fatty acid (SCFA).

You weren't expecting that now, were you? Fat molecules make for unusual knights in shining armor, but in the realm of the GI tract, they are the greatest saviors.

The important role that these tiny molecules play in maintaining health, preventing disease, and healing our battered old bodies makes them the stars of the show. In addition to being the primary source of nutrition for the cells in the colon, they minimize the risk of developing various diseases such as type 2 diabetes, obesity, cardiac problems, and inflammatory diseases.

GETTING TO KNOW THE HERO

Our enigmatic hero's origin story begins in the gut when the good bacteria chance upon an outcast in the large intestine called dietary fiber (indigestible polysaccharides). Instead of abandoning this lonely little fellow, the gentle bacteria decide to take this fiber in, transforming it into SCFAs through anaerobic fermentation. Our gallant warrior decides to leave his hometown and travel to colonocytes (colon cells), where he receives a warm welcome. Colonocytes readily absorb SCFAs, most of which are used as energy sources, while whatever gets left behind is transported to the liver.

SCFAs are crucial for colon health and account for nearly 10% of our daily caloric requirements. They're also necessary for extracting nutrients from carbohydrates and fats. Almost 95% of the SCFAs found in your body consist of acetate, propionate, and butyrate. Propionate plays a prominent role in producing the energy molecule glucose in the small intestine and liver. Acetate is involved in synthesizing lipids (an energy reserve, a vital component of cells, and involved in several important biological functions) and energy production. Lastly, butyrate provides energy for colonocytes (Venegas et al., 2019). Some functions of SCFA that make them crucial for our health are given below.

1. They fortify the epithelial cell barrier and help keep the bad guys out.

2. They strengthen the immune system by activating biological processes inside and outside the cells.

3. They act as a source of energy.

4. They help lower inflammation.

5. They lower our appetite, reducing food intake.

6. They can cross the blood-brain barrier and increase neural growth and development.

7. They stimulate serotonin production in the gut.

8. They improve communication between the gut and the brain.

The amount of SCFAs in your gut is affected by several factors, such as the types of microorganisms residing in your GI tract, the foods you eat, and the time it takes for food to move through your digestive tract.

WHERE DO DIETARY FIBERS COME FROM?

Fiber-rich foods such as fruits, vegetables, and legumes are excellent sources of SCFAs. A recent study involving 153 participants found a positive relationship between eating plant-based foods and higher levels of SCFAs. The research's findings show how the amount of fiber you consume impacts the composition of the gut microbiome (Mueller et al., 2020). Table 1 lists different dietary fibers and the foods in which they're found. Have a look and see if any of these foods are a part of your diet.

TABLE 1

Dietary Fiber	Food Source
Inulin	Artichokes, wheat, rye, garlic, leeks, onions, and asparagus
Fructooligosaccharides	Bananas, asparagus, onions, and garlic
Resistant starch	Grains, legumes, barley, rice, beans, green bananas, and potatoes

Dietary Fiber	Food Source
Pectin	Apples, oranges, apricots, and carrots
Arabinoxylan	Cereal grains such as wheat bran
Guar gum	Guar beans

TWO TO TANGO: GUT MICROBES AND METABOLISM

You're in a fancy restaurant with a friend surrounded by a cacophony of clattering spoons, clinking wine glasses, occasional laughter, and endless chatter of the crowd. The mouthwatering aromas wafting through the kitchen make your stomach growl. You could eat everything!

You glance at your friend and feel a twinge of envy at their lithe, athletic body and toned muscles. Their attire is simple—a black T-shirt over faded jeans, but they manage to turn even the most basic dressing into high street fashion. You glance at your own portly body, sigh, and decide to stick with a salad. When the food arrives, you're shocked by the towering pile of crunchy deep-fried foods in front of your skinny friend.

"I don't believe in diets," they say with a shrug. "I just eat what I like. I guess I have a fast metabolism." (And if this made you clench your teeth, check out Chapter 4, Exercise 3 in the Workbook and unleash your feelings!)

You watch them wolfing down a cheeseburger and look glumly at your sad plate of salad. With another sigh, you grab the fork, curse yourself for missing out on the genetic lottery and jab the innocent floret of broccoli with a little more force than necessary.

Why do some people have this mysterious superpower to eat whatever they want and not gain weight? Is it true that some people simply have a faster metabolism, or is it a myth?

Metabolism is the process, wherein, your body extracts energy from the food you eat. It is a complex process in which the calories packed in foods and beverages are combined with oxygen to produce the energy required for carrying out vital functions such as breathing, blood circulation, hormone production, and the growth and repair of cells. The amount of calories that your body requires to perform these basic functions is called your basal metabolic rate or, quite simply, metabolism.

While genetics does play an important part in how efficiently your body breaks down foods and releases energy, metabolism is also strongly influenced by your lifestyle and health choices. Another factor that can have a significant impact on your metabolism is muscle mass. More muscles mean your metabolism works more efficiently. Moreover, as we age, our metabolism slows down due to a loss of muscle mass (Martin et al., 2019).

What Have Microbes Got To Do With It?

Let's think of our metabolism as one big factory churning out a range of essential products. Microorganisms are the tiny workers that keep the place running by pressing buttons, turning knobs, and pushing levers. Let's find out exactly how they keep the wheels turning.

Short Chain Fatty Acids

Hormones are chemicals manufactured by special cells and organs that travel through your bloodstream to a target cell or organ, where they initiate different processes. They act like little messengers that deliver news about the body to various organs, prompting them to take action. For example, the hormones epinephrine and norepinephrine are released by the adrenal gland when we find ourselves in a stressful, dangerous, or life-threatening situation.

These chemical messengers travel through our body, increasing our heart rate, pumping more blood to the muscles and the brain, relaxing airways, and breaking down sugars to give us a burst of energy. All these processes help us respond quickly to possible dangers and either flee or fight our opponent. Other factors that are controlled by hormones include growth and development, metabolism, sexual arousal, reproduction, and our moods (Martin et al., 2019).

The gut's mucosal lining consists of specialized enteroendocrine (EE) cells, which produce several hormones responsible for a range of physiological functions. The EE cells respond to the nutrients and dietary fibers lining the surface of the gut. The presence of SCFA in the gut triggers the EE cells to produce different gut hormones that are critical for metabolism.

Over the past few years, researchers have stumbled upon several clues that point toward the gut microbiome's impact on metabolism. The bacteria in your gut are believed to influence the EE cells and stimulate hormone production, which can help you feel full, lower stress, and decrease impulsive eating (Martin et al., 2019). Enlisting the help of the tiny workers in your gut can help you stick to your diet, shed pounds, and feel fantastic!

Secondary Bile Acids

Our liver produces a greenish-yellow-colored liquid called bile. Sounds gross, right? Well, I regret to inform or perhaps remind you that it's in your liver right now! And what a job it has to do. This unsightly liquid that you'd rather not hear about breaks down fats and carries away waste products.

It consists of bile acids, which help break down fats and fat-soluble vitamins and assist in their absorption in the small intestine. Microbes metabolize bile acids, producing secondary bile acids, which also signal the EE cells to produce hormones implicated in metabolism (Martin et al., 2019).

Structural Components

The cell contents of bacteria are enclosed inside a membrane that allows the passage of certain molecules while keeping out others. Imagine a plastic bag of water with confetti inside. However, in bacteria, some particles can move across the cell membrane barrier. The membrane that holds everything inside the bacterial cell is made up of lipopolysaccharides (LPS) which bind to toll-like receptors (TLRs). This creates a domino effect that ultimately affects the EE cells and triggers the secretion of metabolically active hormones that can help lower hunger and increase satiety (Martin et al., 2019).

All this shows that metabolism is not something that lies outside our control. Your friend may be blessed with a super fast metabolism that helps them remain active and maintain an ideal weight, but hope is not lost if you don't. Making little tweaks in the gut microbiome allows you to control your metabolism and keep it working efficiently.

DYSBIOSIS AND DISEASE

Now that we know why a balanced microbiome is crucial for our health, let's look at the other side of the coin. What happens when an imbalance occurs in the gut microbiome?

As mentioned previously, countless studies link dysbiosis to various digestive tract diseases. Now, we're going to go deep into what that actually entails. The good and bad bacteria locking horns in your gut not only impact distant organs and cells but also affect colon health. Let's look at some of the issues that arise in the colon following dysbiosis.

Irritable Bowel Syndrome

For many years, researchers have been trying to find the cause of irritable bowel syndrome (IBS). So far, three microorganisms have been found associated with IBS (*Mycobacterium avium paratuberculosis (MAP)*, *Escherichia coli*, and *Clostridium difficile*) (Shariati et al., 2019). However, an overwhelming amount of evidence suggests that IBS could result from dysbiosis rather than a disease caused by a single invading microorganism (Chong et al., 2019).

Symptoms of IBS include abdominal discomfort, bloating, nausea, diarrhea, and constipation. Since antibiotic usage disrupts the microbial balance in the gut, a course of antibiotics can cause IBS (Spiller, 2018). If you've been suffering from symptoms of IBS, ask yourself when was the last time you took antibiotics? Perhaps it was during the time you had a sore throat, or maybe you were prescribed antibiotics following surgery to prevent infection. Ask yourself if it was around this time that your symptoms first turned up.

Symptoms of IBS can appear suddenly following a stomach infection (gastroenteritis) which can sway the balance in the gut in favor of inflammation-causing bacteria, a condition known as post-infectious IBS. Several studies indicate that low levels of inflammation in the musical lining of the gut can snowball into IBS. This is particularly true for people whose IBS doesn't seem to have originated in response to an infection. It is widely believed that changes in the gut microbiome could be the root cause of the inflammation.

Colorectal Cancer

The word cancer is enough to send shivers down anyone's spine. Colorectal cancer is a diagnosis that no one wants to receive; however, it is the third leading cancer in the United States, with a higher prevalence among younger adults. Recent research published in the journal *Cell, Host, and Microbe* discovered an increased number of *Bacteroides fragilis* in colorectal cancer patients (Kordahi et al., 2021).

People suffering from dysbiosis tend to develop polyps in the colon, which may become cancerous. A polyp is a bulbous mass of cells resembling a skin tag that can develop in the colon, ear canal, rectum, or cervix. People with more *Bacteroides fragilis* in the gut are at a higher risk of developing polyps in the colon that may become cancerous.

Inflammatory Bowel Disease (IBD)

A tiny mosquito lands on your forearm and pricks your skin with its sharp needle-like mouth. It takes a long drink of your blood and, once it's had its fill, spreads its wings and takes off, leaving behind a nasty red welt. The itchy red bump the tiny winged visitor leaves behind signifies inflammation.

When a mosquito's proboscis pierces through our skin, our immune system responds to the injury by producing a chemical called histamine. This "tough guy" marches us to the intruders, increasing blood flow to the area and directing immune cells toward the site to fight off the trespassers. Increased blood flow causes redness and warmth in that area while chemicals released by the immune cells leak into the surrounding tissue causing swelling.

The same scenario unfolds underneath our skin in our organs, sometimes due to dysbiosis. Inflammatory bowel disease is a term for two diseases involving inflammation in the GI tract: Crohn's disease and ulcerative colitis. While genetics is a strong indicator, changes in the gut microbiome greatly influence inflammation in the gut, increasing the risk of developing IBD.

Crohn's disease involves damage to the gut lining, which can occur in any part of the GI tract; however, lesions are mostly observed in the small intestine, where they disrupt the absorption of nutrients. In ulcerative colitis, inflammation is restricted to the colon or the large intestine and the rectum (the last part of the large intestine near the anus). In Crohn's disease, the damage penetrates all the layers of the gut lining. In contrast, only the innermost layer of the gut lining is affected by ulcerative colitis (Stewart, 2019).

The medical conditions above are the stuff of nightmares. A healthy lifestyle and a good diet can help us steer clear of these horrible diseases and live a wonderful life. There's a ton of advice coming up to help you avert a looming crisis by maximizing the effect of the good bacteria in your gut. If your body has been showing warning signs of an impending disaster, it's time to start acting now to avoid the catastrophe.

THE GUT-BRAIN AXIS

Ever experienced that strange fluttering sensation in your stomach right before an exam or when you're talking to someone you really like? What gives us butterflies in the pit of our stomachs when we're nervous or excited?

Recent studies show that your gut constantly communicates with your brain and vice versa. Your brain influences what goes on in your gut, and this connection between the two is called the gut-brain axis. The human brain is made up of a complex network of up to 100 billion neurons. However, the number of neurons found in your gut is just as impressive, with 500 million neurons lining the GI tract that make up the enteric nervous system (ENS).

While the ENS is connected to the central nervous system or CNS, composed of the brain and the spinal cord, through a set of nerves (a bundle of fibers that connects the brain to different parts of the body), it can function independently as well. The biggest nerve connecting the gut with the brain is the vagus nerve. It is like the Golden Gate Bridge passing over the shimmering water of the Pacific Ocean, with the mayhem of cars representing the neurons carrying messages.

Communication across the gut-brain axis can be disrupted due to stress. Animal studies have demonstrated the inhibitory effect of stress on signals passing through the vagus nerve and resulting in gastrointestinal problems (Sahar et al., 2001). Imagine huge trucks coming to a halt in the middle of the bridge, blocking traffic and the ensuing chaos. Another study on human subjects detected reduced vagus nerve function in patients suffering from IBS and Crohn's disease (Pellissier et al., 2014).

Another study performed on mice discovered the stress-busting effect of administering probiotics. However, the probiotics had no effect when the vagus nerve was cut, suggesting its importance in the gut-brain axis and its significant role in reducing stress (Bravo et al., 2011).

Filling Up The Feel-Good Hormones

We talked about neurotransmitters in the previous chapter and how they operate a sort of transportation service like Uber inside our body, making sure the electrical messages generated in neurons get where they need to be. Since many of the neurotransmitters are produced in the gut, the GI tract has the ability to influence moods, thoughts, and behaviors.

Most of our body's serotonin (the happiness molecule) is synthesized by the enterochromaffin cells (EC cells) lining the gut, which are activated by the presence of SCFAs. Another essential neurotransmitter called GABA helps us calm down under stressful situations by stopping neurons from firing off. It's the chemical that helps lower anxiety and stress, promote sleep, and reduce blood pressure.

While GABA is primarily produced in the brain from the amino acid, glutamic acid, several gut microbes such as lactic acid bacteria have been found to stimulate the production of calming neurotransmitters by breaking down foods.

Our Body's Fire Department

We discussed inflammation above and the terrifying consequences of prolonged inflammation in the internal organs. While it can develop into serious diseases, it's important to remember that inflammation is our immune system's response to an irritant. Since the gut-brain axis is closely tied with the immune system, microbes can help boost immunity and increase or decrease inflammation.

The bacterial cell membrane is composed of lipopolysaccharides (LPS), which stimulate the production of hormones that impact our metabolism. Damage to the gut barrier causes LPS to seep into the blood, causing unwanted inflammation. In the event that the opposing team of microbes slams our home team, the gut barrier can become compromised, causing LPS to leak into the bloodstream. This can lead to several diseases, including depression, Alzheimer's, dementia, and schizophrenia.

While bad bacteria are busy setting our brain and other organs on fire, SCFAs put on their firefighting gear, jump into their fire engines and barrel toward the inflamed areas. They manage to do so by suppressing the production of immune cells and reducing the secretion of signaling proteins.

From reducing inflammation and fighting off disease-causing microorganisms to boosting our mood and improving our mental well-being, the good microbes living in our gut are ready to defend us at every turn. The only question is: are we ready to join hands with the tiny microbes in our guts in the fight against harmful microorganisms, or are we going to leave them to their own devices and continue taking their numerous health benefits for granted?

Take a moment now with the Workbook. You'll find this chapter's activities very helpful.

IBS: YOUR GUT BACTERIA AFFECT HOW YOUR COLON WORKS!

If there's one thing to know about the human body; it's this: the human body has a ringmaster. This ringmaster controls your digestion, your immunity, your brain, your weight, your health, and even your happiness.
This ringmaster is the gut

—Nancy Mure

You roll out of bed one morning with a tight, uncomfortable feeling in your belly. Your stomach feels like a water balloon that could burst at any moment. The rumbling in your tummy makes you rush to the bathroom, where your body puts up an odious display of sounds and smells. You waddle your way to the kitchen with beads of sweat on your forehead and your skin flushed; a single trip to the bathroom has you worn out.

You pull open the fridge, but just as your outstretched hand reaches for the milk carton, another earthquake jolts your insides, and your hand recoils. You race to the bathroom one more time and listen to your body's orchestra. Just looking at food makes your insides squirm, so you decide to skip breakfast and join the morning traffic on your way to work. Your situation doesn't get any better in the office, and before long, you're shifting in your chair and glancing at the clock, hoping the hands start spinning faster.

You're utterly exhausted by the time you get home. A few bites of your first proper meal of the day awakens the sleeping giant inside you again, and you continue passing wind until night falls and you're lying in bed. Your stomach continues to grumble and growl, making it difficult to fall asleep, and rankish smells emanating from your battle-worn digestive system saturate the air. When the sun comes up, you drag your weary body out of bed and flatulate your way to the bathroom as the cycle repeats itself.

This is the life of people suffering from irritable bowel syndrome (IBS), a disease that affects between 25 and 45 million Americans across all age groups. It is more prevalent in women than men, with about 2 in 3 IBS patients being female. It is estimated that 10-15% of the world population struggles with IBS (International

Foundation for Gastrointestinal Disorders, n.d.). We briefly discussed IBS and its possible causes and symptoms in the previous chapter. However, the global prevalence of the disease warrants further investigation.

IBS is thought to arise when our gut and brain fail to communicate with each other as well as they should. It involves abnormal movement of the colon muscles, affecting how food passes through the large intestine. This makes it a functional disorder because it's caused by the body's inability to carry out normal functions instead of foreign interference such as an attack from a virus.

Some areas in the colon begin to spasm due to certain foods or stress, which can cause the undigested waste to rush down the digestive tract resulting in diarrhea, or it can cause it to slow down, resulting in constipation. People with IBS tend to be more attuned to what's going on in their gut, often experiencing pain from the formation of small gas bubbles, while people with healthy guts don't feel a thing. Strong contractions of the colon muscles can also result in painful cramps.

SYMPTOM CHECKLIST

IBS can trigger utter chaos in your gut. Here are some ways that it affects your body (*Irritable Bowel Syndrome: IBS, Symptoms, Causes, Treatment*, 2020):

- The nerves in the gut become hypersensitive to sensations of pain, a condition known as visceral hypersensitivity.

- The GI muscles can experience abnormal contractions.

- The gut and the brain fail to communicate with each other effectively.

- The immune system can become over or under-active.

The factors above obstruct the colon's normal function, causing a range of symptoms. Look at the IBS signs below and complete Chapter 5, Exercise 1 in the Workbook. Notice if you've been experiencing any of these lately:

1. A change in bowel movements with harder or looser stools than usual.

2. Bloating and excessive gas.

3. White-colored mucus in stools.

Symptoms of IBS may flare up in women during periods. If problems such as abdominal pain and discomfort involved in bowel movements persist for more than six months, you might be suffering from IBS. It's important to note that despite the telltale signs of IBS, everything appears normal during routine tests and examinations.

Based on bowel movement problems, IBS can be divided into three types (Begum, 2021):

- IBS with mixed bowel habits (IBS-M)

- IBS with constipation (IBS-C)

- IBS with diarrhea (IBS-D)

CAUSES OF IBS

So far, experts have been unable to pin down an exact cause for IBS; however, it is widely accepted in scientific circles that the condition is a combination of more than one problem. The disease could manifest in different people due to a number of varied reasons. Functional disorders such as IBS usually arise due to issues along the gut-brain axis. Communication misfires between the brain and the gut, affect normal processes in the GI tract, and may cause IBS (Begum, 2021).

One theory that has been gaining widespread attention is that IBS could result from an imbalance of serotonin. People with too much serotonin in their guts end up with diarrhea, while those with too little suffer from constipation; however, serotonin-induced mood swings are common in both scenarios (Begum, 2021). Some researchers believe a wide variety of problems ranging from psychological issues to genetics could lead to the development of IBS, such as

1. Traumatic early life experiences.

2. Depression or other mental health issues.

3. Bacterial infections in the GI tract.

4. Dysbiosis.

5. Food intolerance.

6. Genetic predisposition toward developing IBS.

7. Diet rich in protein and carbs.

SEARCHING FOR ANSWERS IN THE GUT MICROBIOME

Let's put on our imagination hats and visualize ourselves as tiny little humans wearing climbing harnesses and clambering down the dark GI tract. We land with a soft padding sound and turn on our flashlights. We see the gut seething with Firmicutes and Bacteroidetes and plunging numbers of our home team bacteria, Lactobacilli and Bifidobacteria. The mutinous bacteria running amok start breaking the epithelial barrier. Our home team bacteria try to fix the damage, but they don't have the numbers to overpower the rebels.

We see the miscreants puncture holes in the epithelial barrier, increasing intestinal permeability, a phenomenon known as leaky gut. The fiendish bacteria begin climbing through these perforations, escaping the GI tract and entering the bloodstream. The breakout doesn't go unnoticed by the immune system, and now we can hear a crescendo of sirens as immune cells come speeding toward the gut. This causes the gut to become inflamed, leading to IBS or IBD.

Meanwhile, some of the rioters begin tampering with the movement of the gut muscles. We know that genes are a set of instructions that tell different organs of our body how to function. Some dissident bacteria, such as *Bacteroides thetaiotaomicron*, change the written instructions for gut movement, causing it to malfunction. Others such as *Escherichia coli* directly stimulate the colon muscles causing painful contractions. The wily bacteria also tinker with the Enteric Nervous System (ENS), increasing pain perception (Distrutti et al., 2016).

Our trip to the gut comes to an end. We've witnessed the ruckus caused by a few renegade microbes, and we're ready to leave. We climb up the GI tract and exit through the mouth. Now that we've magically restored ourselves to our normal size, it's time to ask ourselves: what could we do to repair the damage in our gut?

A ceasefire between the warring bacteria to end our agony seems like the only solution—if only we could bring some microbes to wave the white flag and broker a peace deal. Luckily, this book will teach you how to do just that. As you read through the following chapters, you'll learn how you can recruit beneficial bacteria to fight on your side and quell the rebellion.

There's nothing quite as awful as not feeling in control of your own body. IBS can rob you of your social life and make you feel like a stranger in your own skin. The microbial circus inside your gut can have far-reaching consequences, but you have the power to stop the mayhem and restore peace and harmony to the gut microbiome.

6

INFLAMMATION: AN IMMUNE RESPONSE FROM THE GUT

Your gut is not Las Vegas. What happens in the gut does not stay in the gut.

—Dr. Peter Kozlowski, M.D.

We briefly discussed inflammation in the previous chapter. In this chapter, we will look at inflammation in more detail and learn about chronic inflammation and its devastating effects. Before we deep dive into the issue, let's do a quick recap of what inflammation is.

Inflammation occurs when your body fights off disease, reacts to injury, or detects toxins. It is the body's attempt to heal itself. The immune cells patrolling through your body release chemicals in response to the aforementioned triggers. These chemicals signal the immune system to send backup and launch a full-scale attack on the invaders. As a result, blood rushes to the site of injury along with antibodies and proteins. If the process lasts a few hours or a couple of days, it's called acute inflammation. This is usually the case when we suffer a minor injury like a cut or catch a cold.

In some scenarios, the immune response persists for a long time, keeping your body in a state of high alert. This is known as chronic inflammation, which can have dire consequences. While signs of acute inflammation are fairly obvious (for example, a red hump after an insect bite or a swollen ankle after twisting it), symptoms of chronic inflammation are not so apparent.

CHRONIC INFLAMMATION

There is nothing quite as annoying as the screech of a smoke detector gone rogue. The high-pitched noise is meant to catch your attention and can be potentially life-saving, but it's extremely aggravating if the alarm keeps going off for no reason. Chronic inflammation is your body's alarm system going haywire.

The First Responders

The chain of events leading to chronic inflammation is similar to acute inflammation. Once the immune response is activated, the blood vessels expand (vasodilation), causing rapid blood flow to the damaged area. This is accompanied by the increase in permeability of the capillaries (tiny blood vessels covering tissues, muscles, and nerves), which allows first responders (immune cells) to pass through the blood to the target site easily.

The key difference between acute and chronic inflammation lies in the type of immune cells that cross over from the blood to the concerned area. The immune cells that reach the site of injury immediately after the alarm goes off are short-lived cells called neutrophils; other inflammatory cells (the macrophages and lymphocytes) hop over soon afterward.

The macrophages and lymphocytes begin replacing neutrophils and start infiltrating the tissue site secreting a wide array of inflammatory molecules such as cytokines, plasma cells, and growth factors. The growing concentrations of inflammatory molecules lead to tissue damage, scarring, and the formation of granulomas (a small nodule created by a mass of immune cells) (Pahwa et al., 2022).

Cause Of Chronic Inflammation

Chronic inflammation can arise due to several reasons, some of which are listed below:

- An untreated case of acute inflammation such as an infection or injury. For example, infectious agents such as bacteria, fungi, or viruses can sometimes evade our defense system, dwelling in the tissues for a long time.

- Exposure to low concentrations of irritants such as silica dust, which our body cannot break down and remove from our system.

- Autoimmune disorders such as rheumatoid arthritis and systemic lupus erythematosus trick the immune system into attacking healthy tissue.

- The inability of anti-inflammatory cells to lower inflammation due to a defect. For example, an auto-inflammatory disorder such as the familial Mediterranean fever.

- Recurring instances of acute inflammation.

Who's At Risk?

A specific set of characteristics increases the probability of developing chronic inflammation (Pahwa et al., 2022). Habits and attributes that promote a low-level inflammatory response include

- **Age:** An uptick in the production of inflammatory molecules as we age puts older individuals at a higher risk of developing inflammation.

- **Obesity:** Excessive fat tissue produces multiple inflammatory substances, causing elevated levels of inflammation.

- **Diet:** Eating foods rich in trans fats, saturated fats, and refined sugars leads to pro-inflammatory molecule build-up, placing overweight individuals and diabetics at a greater risk of suffering from chronic inflammation.

- **Smoking:** Cigarette smoke can induce inflammation by suppressing the production of anti-inflammatory substances.

- **Stress and Sleep Problems:** Emotional and physical stress stimulates the release of cytokines (cell signaling molecules that initiate an inflammatory response). Lack of sleep can cause stress levels to rise, mounting up inflammation.

What Are The Warning Signs?

Symptoms of chronic inflammation are sometimes so subtle they can easily slip under our radar (Pahwa et al., 2022). Common signs to look out for include:

- Abdominal and chest pain.

- Chronic fatigue.

- Insomnia.

- Mental health issues such as anxiety, depression, and mood swings.

- Frequent problems related to the GI tract such as constipation, diarrhea, or acid reflux.

- Weight fluctuations.

- Skin problems such as rashes or psoriasis.

Still confused about whether you have chronic inflammation or not? If the answer is yes, head over to Chapter 6, Exercise 3 of the Workbook, and have a go at the exercise designed to help you gain clarity over your symptoms.

Consequences Of Chronic Inflammation

The diseases associated with chronic inflammation can be potentially life-threatening. Some estimates suggest that 3 of 5 people worldwide die due to chronic inflammatory diseases such as stroke, cancer, chronic respiratory diseases, and cardiac problems. Some diseases linked to chronic inflammation include

- Diabetes

- Cardiovascular diseases

- Rheumatoid arthritis

- Allergies such as hay fever

- Respiratory disorders such as asthma

- Cognitive problems such as dementia

DIAGNOSIS

There are no specific diagnostic tests for detecting chronic inflammation alone. It is usually diagnosed in connection to other medical conditions. Certain blood tests used to identify other diseases can serve as good markers. For example, detecting the presence of C-reactive protein (CRP) to identify rheumatoid arthritis and high-sensitivity C-reactive protein (hs-CRP), which points toward inflammation of the heart, may indicate the presence of chronic inflammation.

FINDING THE CULPRITS IN THE GUT

The underlying cause of chronic inflammation can be traced back to the gut. The GI tract is not only home to the human microbiome, it is also the place where 70% of the immune cells reside (Fields, n.d.). The bad bacteria in the gut are like hooligans that pull the fire alarm for fun, activating the immune system and causing the immune cells to come careering toward the site.

The gut microbiome works in tandem with the immune system to ensure that trespassers are taken care of, and our body is protected. As I mentioned in the previous chapters, the microbes in the gut act as gatekeepers and coaches for the immune cells. They help keep the bad guys out and teach immune cells to distinguish between our own cells and foreign entities.

When things are going swimmingly, the gut regulates immune responses by creating a healthy and robust immune system. In return, the immune system helps beneficial bacteria thrive in the gut. We learned in the previous chapters how communication misfires along the gut-brain axis could impact the immune system, leading to a number of diseases. Since the gut-brain axis is heavily dependent on the gut microbiome, the intestinal flora shares a close connection with our immune system.

Factors that lower bacterial diversity in the gut can weaken the immune system, leaving us vulnerable to various health problems. An unhealthy diet, exposure to heavy metals, chemotherapy, and antibiotics can cause bacterial populations in the gut to plummet, lowering immunity. An ambitious new study published in the journal *Gut* explored the effect of 173 dietary factors on the microbiome of 1425 participants.

The researchers singled out animal food products, grain-based, processed, and sugary foods as the real culprit for egging on bad bacteria in the gut to produce excessive amounts of inflammation. But don't worry, there's some good news to go along with that doom and gloom! The study findings also discovered that a plant-based diet tends to have the opposite effect on the GI tract by curbing inflammation and enhancing the gatekeeping function of the microbiome (Bolte et al., 2021).

You must be curious to meet the hoodlum bacteria that run around the gut, causing a ruckus. Let's line up the suspects so we can have a good look at the miscreants. We've met some of these microbial bandits in the previous chapters, while some are entirely new. Increased intake of animal-derived, grain-based, processed, and sugary foods cause *Firmicutes* and *Ruminococcus* populations in the gut to grow, resulting in a spike in inflammation.

Chomping down lots of meat, mayonnaise, french fries, and chugging bottles of soda causes the population of inflammation-causing bacteria such as *Clostridium bolteae*, *Coprobacillus*, and *Lachnospiraceae* to soar. Some bacteria are more shrewd than others and only promote inflammation under certain conditions. Scientists term these bacteria " opportunistic." These include species such as *Oscillibacter* that begin feeding on the gut's epithelial lining when they are deprived of dietary fibers (Guite & Butler, 2021).

TURNING DOWN THE HEAT

By now, we've established the crucial role of gut bacteria in causing inflammation. We looked at the signs and symptoms of chronic inflammation, the risk factors, and the dietary habits that could be provoking the bacteria in our gut to turn up the heat. We briefly looked at some of the dreadful problems that patients with chronic inflammation can run into and some foods that could put our immune system on a collision course with the gut microbiome.

Luckily, there are ways to turn our body's thermostat down and avert imminent disaster. In the upcoming chapters, we will focus on finding solutions and fill you up with the information you need to make the right decisions for your health. We will learn why the vegetable and fruit aisle at your local supermarket could hold the elixir of health and the steps you can turn over a new leaf.

WEIGHT GAIN: HOW YOUR GUT IS TO BLAME FOR THE EXTRA POUNDS

No crash diet or hot trend can replace consistently making good choices.

— Renée Jones

A few years ago, when I was at the lowest point in my life due to my deteriorating health, I remember glancing at the mirror and feeling ashamed of my appearance. I did not like the way I looked. I felt a pang of embarrassment whenever I'd catch a glimpse of my reflection, so I started avoiding mirrors at all costs, since it was the only solution I could think of to lower my distress.

In a few months, I had reached my highest weight ever. My self-esteem crumbled when I could no longer fit in the clothes in my closet. My growing insecurity about my looks made me timid and withdrawn. I shut myself off from my family and friends and felt unmotivated to pursue my dreams. It didn't take me long to realize that I couldn't go on living like that much longer. I had to get my life back on track. I needed to feel good about myself, and, for that, I needed to lose weight.

I tried every diet under the sun to shave off some pounds, but my attempts proved a dismal failure. I would lose some weight initially, but I'd bounce back to my original weight after a few weeks. The yo-yo effect left me feeling exhausted. *If only I could find a way to keep my weight stable.*

My light bulb moment happened while I was researching the role of gut bacteria on human health. I realized that most diets inevitably failed to keep the weight off because they ignored a vital component of our body: the gut microbiome.

I know firsthand how hard it can be to lose weight, especially since guilt, shame, and embarrassment are quintessential parts of the weight loss journey. I remember wallowing in self-loathing for days after having a minor slip-up—a cupcake that was too hard to resist or a doughnut that was practically screaming at me to eat it with that chocolate glaze and those sprinkles. I'd feel miserable whenever I failed to stick to my strict diet, yet I couldn't stop myself from giving in to my sugar cravings.

Struggling with your weight can make you feel isolated at times. Here's what you need to remember when you're down in the dumps: you're not alone. Obesity rates around the globe have increased threefold since 1975. In 2016, the number of overweight adults surpassed 1.9 billion. A recent study conducted in 30 countries found that 45% of people are trying to lose weight worldwide (Ipsos, 2021).

While it is hard sometimes to lose the extra pounds and return to your ideal weight, consistently making the right decisions will ultimately help you achieve your goal. Calorie-counting, kicking carbs, and extensive exercise is useless if we don't consider the microorganisms in our gut.

WHY WEIGHT LOSS ISN'T ONE SIZE FITS ALL

As you embark on your weight loss journey, you're bound to hear doctors, personal trainers, or diet coaches use terms you might be unfamiliar with. So let's start off by understanding some of the scientific gibberish that will get thrown your way.

Two words that you might be sick of hearing by now are obesity and Body Mass Index or BMI. What makes people decide who's obese and who's not, and what does your BMI have to do with it? The World Health Organization (WHO) defines obesity "as abnormal or excessive fat accumulation that may impair health."

People can be classified as being overweight or obese using the body mass index (BMI), which calculates their weight-to-height ratio by dividing their weight in kilograms by the square of their height in meters (kg/m2). Generally, a BMI of 30 or higher indicates obesity, while a BMI of less than 18 falls within the underweight range (World Health Organization, 2021).

Another term that you're bound to run into is body composition, which refers to the amount of fat, bones, and muscles in your body. Health and fitness experts use this term to find the percentage of fat in your body, which helps them figure out how healthy you are. Body composition can sometimes create a strange conundrum when two people with the same body mass index have different fat percentages.

So, someone who's the same height and weight as you may not suffer from the same health issues or risk of disease based on the amount of muscle and fat inside them. This is what makes weight loss tricky sometimes. Stepping on the scales won't give you an idea about the fat or muscle mass percentage inside your body. But, wait! Don't chuck the weighing scale out the window just yet.

Determining body composition is not so simple. Health professionals may use different methods to calculate the amount of body fat inside an individual. These include using skin calipers to measure skin fold thickness, underwater weighing, and performing dual x-ray absorptiometry (DEXA) scans. Meanwhile, bioelectrical impedance measures fat content by sending weak electrical currents through the body and noting the rate at which it travels (Ratini, 2021). Don't freak out; you don't have to get any of that done!

You'll find it much easier to stay motivated if you keep body composition in mind. For example, most people become disheartened when they run into a weight loss plateau: when they stop losing weight despite following a strict diet plan and exercise regimen. Body composition tells us that even if you stop losing weight during this time, you could be gaining muscle mass.

Energy balance is another concept that gets tossed around a lot. Fitness gurus and diet coaches will have you believe weight loss is as simple as burning more calories than you consume. However, energy intake and expenditure depend on several factors, making this process more complicated than it seems. The energy balance equation looks like this:

Energy balance = energy intake - energy expenditure

As long as the energy we consume stays equal to the energy we expend, our weight remains stable. When energy intake trumps energy expenditure, we gain weight. When we use more energy than we consume, the balance tilts in favor of weight loss. The above equation reinforces the common belief: "*Eat less, move more.*" Sounds simple, right?

Here's the catch: not everyone's body responds to the excess or deficit of energy in the same way. Ideally, if your energy consumption exceeds the amount your body requires by 3,500 calories, you could gain one pound. The opposite happens when your energy intake falls short by 3,500 calories, and your body breaks down stored fat to fulfill its energy needs. However, an important factor can distort the above formula. The crucial component that can skew the energy balance is tucked away deep inside us.

The Hidden Factor

The mysterious element that can significantly impact your weight is basal metabolic energy (BMR). Let's look at exactly what it is and how it can influence weight loss.

The total amount of energy that we use depends on three crucial aspects:

1. Basal metabolic rate

2. Thermic effect of food (the energy required for digestion)

3. Physical activity

The energy used up when our body is at rest is BMR. It is the amount of energy required to fuel behind-the-scenes activities such as respiration, blood circulation, protein synthesis, and temperature regulation. For a person living a sedentary lifestyle, a vast bulk of the energy is used up by the body to execute everyday biological functions, meaning BMR makes up about 60 to 75% of the total energy expenditure. For example, BMR might take up 1200 calories per day from a total calorie intake of 1800 in a sedentary person.

BMR depends largely on a person's lean body mass, which comprises organs, bones, and muscles. This means BMR can vary greatly among people of different sizes, gender, and medical conditions. Table 2 shows various facets that influence BMR. Go through the list and check if any of these apply to you (Powell, n.d.).

Increase BMR	Decrease BMR
More lean body mass	Less lean body mass
Large body frame	Small body frame
Young age	Old age
Male gender	Female gender
High levels of thyroid hormone	Low levels of thyroid hormone
Stress	Fasting or starvation
Health problems	
Pregnancy or breastfeeding	

Now that we know where the energy gained from food is spent, let's look at what causes hunger pangs in the first place.

WHAT MAKES US FEEL HUNGRY?

It's the first day of your diet, and you wake up feeling ready. You've resolved to lose weight a couple of times before and given up, but this time things will be different. You start your day off with some poached eggs and some fruits, then go on a brisk morning walk. You feel good about yourself when you return and glance at the clock before jumping into the shower. You're supposed to have your next meal around noon, and you've got a handful of almonds to munch on until then.

You step out of the shower and get dressed, humming a happy tune. A loud growl startles you, and you give the room a wide-eyed once over. *There's that sound again.* You look down at your stomach and hear its protestations loud and clear. This time the grumbling is accompanied by an uncomfortable sensation. You toughen up and munch on a few almonds to make it go away, but your grumbling tummy won't leave you alone, and food is all that you can think about!

So, what's really going on in our stomachs, and what's with all the noise?

A small region in the brain called the hypothalamus is responsible for hunger cues such as stomach growling, exhaustion, trouble focusing, and headaches. The hypothalamus generates feelings of hunger or satiety by detecting the level of nutrients in our blood. As I mentioned in the previous chapters, our gut and brain are constantly talking with each other. When nutrient levels fall, the gut signals to the brain: *"Hey, I could really use a burger right now."*

The brain responds:

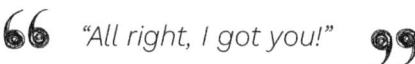 *"All right, I got you!"*

And the next thing you know, you're in your car, driving toward McDonald's.

The grumbling noise that comes from your stomach when you're feeling hungry is due to stomach contractions when it is empty. We don't hear the same sounds when we're full because the food inside our stomach muffles the noise. An empty stomach also releases the "hunger hormone" called ghrelin. Production of this hormone amps up before a meal and drops once nutrient levels in the blood rise. Once you've eaten, the stomach stretches, which sends neural messages to the brain, triggering feelings of satiety. *"That's enough,"* the brain tells us, and we place our fork and spoon down, dab our mouths with a napkin, and beckon the waiter to bring us our bill.

The gastrointestinal tract, pancreas, and adipose tissues (body fat) secrete hormones that make us feel full. Cholecystokinin (CCK) is one such hormone that induces satiety and is secreted in response to the concentration of nutrients in the gut, including fat and protein content. Additionally, CCK activates the production of hormones in the pancreas, causes gall bladder contractions, and increases intestinal movements—all of which assist in the digestion of food and absorption of nutrients.

Fat tissue is another body component that plays a prominent role in regulating food intake by producing the hormone leptin, which sates our appetite, suppresses hunger, and stimulates energy expenditure. The discovery of this hormone and its various functions attracted interest from many researchers, resulting in a focus on diet pills. It was believed that administering leptin to obese people could help curb their appetite.

However, over time, several clinical trials disproved this myth, with overwhelming evidence indicating that people struggling with obesity are resistant to leptin. This means their brain does not respond to it the same way. Instead of making them put down the fork and push their plate away, the signal is ignored by their brain, and they go on eating (Powell, n.d.).

TRUST YOUR GUT TO LOSE WEIGHT

Wouldn't it be great if you had a magic wand that you could wave and make all the excess body fat disappear? During my battle with weight loss, I'd often fantasize about waking up one morning and realizing that my body had shrunk back to my ideal weight! You can imagine my disappointment when I'd roll out of bed looking exactly the same as the day before.

While there's no magic spell to make you thin overnight, the little helpers inside your gut can smooth out your weight loss journey and increase your chances of success. We've established in the previous chapters that the gut microbiome influences hunger, satiety, and our moods to a great degree, but can these tiny microbes help speed up weight loss?

The idea that the tiny helpers in our gut could help us lose weight encouraged scientists to probe further. Christian Diener and his team at the Institute of Systems Biology in Seattle analyzed certain bacterial genes to determine whether specific gut bacteria are more capable of helping people lose weight. They looked at genes that controlled microbial growth, nutrient extraction, and digestion of starches and fibers.

One study compared the gut microbiome of people who lost weight each month with the microbiome of people whose weight remained constant and found differences in 31 genes. The study's findings reaffirmed the belief that various gut bacteria could influence weight loss interventions (Diener et al., 2021).

Fast-growing bacteria were found to be capable of aiding weight loss because they used more nutrients from food, leaving behind a small quantity, which could contribute to weight gain. Some evidence suggests that a common gut bacteria called Prevotella are among some of the fastest-growing microbes and helps significantly in weight loss.

In contrast, slow-growing bacteria that secrete more enzymes to break down fibers and starches into sugars are thought to impede weight loss (McNamara, 2021). For example, the GI tracts of people who consume more animal protein and fat are crowded with Bacteroidetes. A recent study examined the role of these two bacteria in weight loss by giving a high-fiber, whole grain diet to 62 people for 26 weeks. The results showed that people who had more Prevotella lost more body fat than people who had more Bacteroidetes (Hjorth et al., 2018).

Now that we know some players on our home team and our opposing team, let's take a step back and round up the different elements influenced by the gut microbiome, as they're inextricably linked to our body weight.

Factors Affected By The Gut Microbiome

- Gut bacteria digest flavonoids (plant pigments), preventing weight gain.

- They affect fat absorption in the intestine and its storage in the body.

- Some bacteria increase inflammation, leading to weight gain.

- Healthy bacteria produce SCFAs that can stimulate the production of hormones that induce satiety and suppress hunger.

- They influence our mood by stimulating serotonin synthesis and can impact stress-induced eating.

Losing weight can be challenging. Luckily, when equipped with the right tools and knowledge, along with some determination, you can reach your goals. Learning about your gut microbiome can help ensure that the next time you look in the mirror, you're overflowing with self-love.

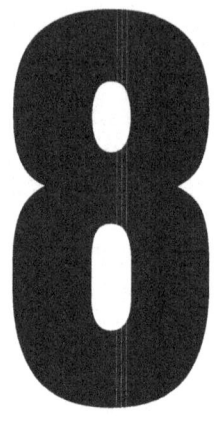

HERE'S HOW DYSBIOSIS COULD BE KEEPING YOU AWAKE

Let food be thy medicine and medicine be thy food.

— Hippocrates
Greek physician 460 - 370 BC

You toss and turn on the bed at night, hoping you'll find a position that's comfortable enough to make you doze off, but sleep continues to evade you. You curl up on your side, punch your pillow and squeeze your eyes shut once more. A hundred sheep have hopped over the fence so far in your head, but sleep remains a distant memory. Before you know it, sunlight is pouring in from the window, and you can hear the birds tweeting outside. You drag yourself out of your bed and shuffle to the bathroom with bleary eyes.

You join the morning traffic with a scowl on your face. Everything seems a little too bright and a little too loud: the honking cars, the tailpipes puffing smoke, the blazing sun, and the barking dog— *everything grates on your nerves.* You make it to your office, flop on the chair, and begin punching the keyboard. Before long, your phone's ringing, and you're bombarded with emails and flooded with stacks of files. *Has everyone always been this annoying?*

You snap, grumble and grind your teeth as you plow through the day and finally slouch your way home. At night, you crawl into bed feeling bone-tired. The moonlight filters in from the window, and you lie awake watching the shadows on the ceiling. Meanwhile, the ruthless microbes in your gut snicker as they succeed in tormenting you in yet another way.

GUT MICROBES AND SLEEP DEPRIVATION: HOW DO THEY DO IT?

We discussed in the gut-brain previous chapters. Let's take a quick look at how the gut communicates with our brain and how that could be the reason we're unable to grab some shut-eye.

If you recall from earlier in this book, the gut-brain axis is a two-way communication channel between your brain (Central Nervous System) and your gut (Enteric Nervous System). It connects our emotional and cognitive systems with intestinal functions through a complex network of nerves.

Different communication pathways exist between the microbiome and the brain, linking gastrointestinal problems and mood disorders. These include the endocrine, immune and neuronal pathways. For example, the secretion of stress hormones such as cortisol, cytokines, and neural messages carried along the vagus, ENS, and spinal nerves are involved in relaying information along the gut-brain axis.

Moreover, many gut microbes produce neurotransmitters such as GABA, noradrenaline, dopamine, and serotonin, which open an important communication channel with the brain. In addition, these microbes synthesize metabolites such as SCFAs that can influence our thoughts and behaviors.

Chapter 4 touched on the vagus nerve and how it acts like the Golden Gate Bridge connecting the brain and the gut. The vagus nerve is one of the 12 cranial nerves connecting the brain to different body parts. It originates from the brain stem and ends at the colon, making it the longest cranial nerve.

Based on their function, cranial nerves can be divided into three groups: sensory, motor, and nerves that are involved in both. Sensory nerves send signals associated with sensations such as sights, sounds, smell, and taste, while motor nerves control muscle movements and the function of glands and organs.

However, some nerves, like the vagus nerve, perform both functions.

Some tasks that the vagus nerve is in charge of include stimulating the heart muscles and gut peristalsis. Increased immune cell activity in the gut can cause the vagus nerve in that area to become inflamed, a condition known as enteric neuroinflammation, which can cause anxiety, depression, Alzheimer's, and Parkinson's. Moreover, chronic inflammation of the gut has also been linked to mental health problems such as depression. In many cases, the inflammation is caused by the circulation of bacterial components called lipopolysaccharides (LPS). So, while it may not seem apparent, problems in the brain—including insomnia— often arise due to the microorganisms housed in the gut.

The Gut Clock

I remember traveling from New York to Australia for a vacation once and experiencing horrible jet lag. My plane left New York at around 9 p.m. on Monday, and I arrived in Sydney at 11 a.m. on Tuesday. I stifled a yawn and rubbed my tired eyes in my hotel room, which was filled with bright sunlight, and spent the next few days feeling the most alert at night.

There's an invisible clock fixed inside our body that regulates our daily activities, appetite, and sleep. We can't hear it tick, but we can observe its effects on our bodies. This internal clock makes up our circadian rhythm, which marks mental, physical, and behavioral changes that take place in us over a 24-hour cycle.

Jet lag occurs anytime we travel across two or more time zones, and our internal clock gets out of sync with the new time zone.

Our biological clock controls when we go to sleep and wake up. We start feeling sleepy when it is dark because our body produces a compound called melatonin, which helps us fall asleep. When the sun rises, our brain switches off melatonin production, and we feel wide awake and alert. However, gut bacteria can mess with our biological clock and disrupt our natural sleep-wake cycle, making our lives miserable.

Microbial populations in the gut ebb and flow during different times in the day, showing the close link between the gut microbiome and our biological clock. For example, Bacteroidetes and Firmicutes populations, which represent 99% of the gut microbiome, peak and drop at various times during the day. Moreover, several experiments conducted on germ-free and antibiotic-treated mice showed that changes in circadian rhythms could influence microbial populations in the gut.

In addition, researchers found that jet lag and working long hours at night can affect the microbial composition in the gut. Several studies have analyzed the changes in the relationship between the gut microbiome, circadian rhythms, and the brain influence disease risk and severity. Placing animals in light or dark conditions for 24 hours wiped out gut microbes, leading to weight gain and glucose intolerance when they were given a high-fat diet (Guglielmi, 2020).

Similarly, microbes in the gut can alter circadian rhythms by changing the concentration of metabolites such as SCFAS and bile acids. When SCFAs were orally administered to antibiotic-treated mice, scientists observed changes in gene expression, which impacted their biological clock. Researchers also witnessed changes in the circadian rhythm genes in cells cultured in a lab dish in response to bile acids.

Dysbiosis Could Be Stressing You Out

By mediating the production of neurotransmitters such as serotonin and dopamine and stress-inducing hormones such as epinephrine, norepinephrine, and cortisol, gut bacteria can lift our mood or crush our spirits. Let's look at how the tiny gut microbes could be keeping you high-strung.

Imagine coming across a large, terrifying dog on your otherwise uneventful morning walk. The dog bares its sharp teeth and lets out a low growl. Your heart races, your palms sweat, and your mind goes into a frenzy as you try to decide whether to run or stand your ground.

When we venture into a dangerous situation, our hypothalamus (a region in our brain that we discussed in the previous chapter) prepares us to either fight the enemy or bolt. A combination of hormone and nerve signals directs the adrenal gland, present on top of your kidneys, to produce a surge of hormones such as adrenaline (epinephrine and norepinephrine) and cortisol.

Adrenaline makes your heart pound faster, increases blood pressure, and jacks up energy supplies. Meanwhile, cortisol increases blood sugar levels, boosts the brain's use of glucose, and speeds up tissue repair. Cortisol also makes sure we don't waste our energy on non-essential processes. For example, it changes our immune system responses and curbs the energy consumed by the digestive system, the reproductive system, and growth processes.

The stress response above is generally self-limiting, with hormone levels declining and returning to normal once the danger has passed. Imagine the dog you felt so frightened of, lowering its head and coming forward to lick your hand. The cortisol and adrenaline pumping through your body nosedive when you realize you're not under attack. Your heart rate and blood pressure would drop to baseline levels and the other systems, which were put on pause, begin to kick in.

If the switch that turns our stress response on and off gets broken, our body remains in a constant state of fight-or-flight even in the absence of any perceived threat. This is essentially the same as putting on your boxing gear and trying to fight your own shadow on the wall. A malfunctioning stress response system can lead to serious health risks such as anxiety, depression, digestive issues, weight gain, cardiac diseases, and (you guessed it!) sleep problems.

With stress levels at an all-time high, it's nearly impossible to get a good night's sleep. The bacteria in your gut can trick your brain into producing stress hormones through common gut-brain communication pathways such as neurotransmitters and the release of peptide hormones from the gut. The neurotransmitters and gut peptides bind to receptors on the surface of immune cells and vagus nerve terminals, activating the stress response. Moreover, research suggests a close connection between the gut microbiome and the hypothalamic-pituitary-adrenal (HPA) axis: those parts of the brain that regulate the stress response (The Microbiome, Stress Hormones, & Gut Function, n.d.).

The concentrations of these signaling molecules change in response to varying microbial populations in the gut. Several studies, including a 2019 article published in *Frontiers in Genetics* (Huang et al., 2019), suggest that:

- Major depressive disorder (MDD) is linked to changes in gut permeability (leaky gut) and microbial composition.

- Patients suffering from GI disorders like IBS experience more frequent episodes of anxiety and depression.

- Gastrointestinal disorders such as colitis, Crohn's disease, and dyspepsia have also been linked to negative emotions, stressful events, and personality disorders such as neuroticism.

The microbes in your gut could be to blame for your short temper, lack of sleep, and anxiety, but they don't have to keep running the show any longer. By switching to a plant-based diet and adopting the strategies outlined in the upcoming chapters, you can turn the tables and make the bad bacteria in your gut run for cover as your home team takes over.

BLOATING: A CLEAR (AND HELPFUL!) SIGN OF AN UNHEALTHY GUT

The doctor of the future will no longer treat the human frame with drugs, but rather will cure and prevent disease with nutrition.

— Thomas Edison
Inventor of the light bulb

You eat a meal and . . .

Poof!

You blow up like a pufferfish.

The taut feeling in your abdomen makes you reach under the dinner table and discreetly unbutton your pants, so you can get some room to breathe. *It's uncomfortable. It's embarrassing.* And it's the perfect ingredient for whipping up some of the most awkward moments in your life as you fight the urge to belch in public to relieve your discomfort. I know; I've been there. So let's talk about the elephant in the room (no pun intended).

Bloating happens when the abdominal pressure on the gut increases due to gas build-up. Common symptoms of bloating include abdominal distension (a bulging tummy), flatulence, and abdominal discomfort. While everyone experiences bloating occasionally after overindulging during the holidays, the problem arises when you experience it frequently.

WHAT'S CAUSING IT?

Some reasons that you could make you bloated include:

- Small Intestinal Bacterial Overgrowth (SIBO): Increased levels of bacteria in the small intestine.

- Dysbiosis: Microbial imbalance in the gut following antibiotic treatments, unhealthy diet, or other reasons.

- Food intolerance: Inability to digest certain foods.

- Hyper sensitivity: Increased perception of changes in the digestive tract.

- Lumbar lordosis: Increase in the curvature of the spine's lumbar area. This decreases the space in the abdomen, reducing its capacity to hold gas.

- Gastroparesis: Slow movement of food through the GI tract due to decreased contractions of the gut.

- Additional reasons: Coeliac disease, gastrointestinal infections, hormonal imbalances, and IBS.

WHERE DOES ALL THAT GAS COME FROM?

Humans produce a lot of gas! Nearly one and half-pints of methane, hydrogen, and carbon dioxide are emitted daily. But where does all this gas come from? We know by now that our microbiome assists digestion, making sure that all the food is broken down. Gas is released as a natural byproduct of this process. If the amount of these gasses exceeds normal levels, we start suffering from problems such as bloating.

While suffering from excessive gas certainly feels awful, it can be a sign of digestive problems brewing inside our gut. Despite the many scientific breakthroughs we've made over the past few decades, there's no way for us to tell what's going on in our gut until symptoms appear (check out Chapter 9, Exercise 1 of the Workbook). So, if you find yourself complaining about feeling full and gassy more often than the people around you, it could indicate a shift in the microbial balance in your gut.

Low Stomach Acid

The GI tract, especially the large intestine, is loaded with trillions of bacteria. The microbiome is essential for carrying out many useful tasks such as breaking down food, absorbing nutrients, and assisting the immune system. When harmful bacteria manage to dominate the gut microbiome, these processes get disrupted, leading to multifarious problems. In some instances, bloating arises because of low stomach acid. Let's take a quick look at digestion and see where things could be going wrong.

The food we eat lands in our stomach, where it is digested by muscular contractions and the action of stomach acids. Stomach walls are lined with gastric glands that pump hydrochloric acid to help break down food. The release of hydrochloric acid activates the enzyme pepsin, which targets protein content in the food. Once the volume of stomach acid reaches a certain level, bile and pancreatic enzymes are released into the intestine to finish the job by digesting any remaining food content.

Plunging stomach acid levels can disrupt food digestion, causing upper abdominal bloating. While stomach acid levels gradually fall with age, certain medications, chronic stress, and improper chewing can cut back production. Gastrointestinal infections from bacteria such as *Helicobacter pylori*, the causative agent of stomach ulcers, can also contribute to a significant drop in stomach acid content. Falling levels of hydrochloric acid levels cause tiny holes to appear in the intestinal lining, leading to a leaky gut.

Since hydrochloric acid also keeps the bacterial population in check, decreasing levels of stomach acid can lead to small intestinal bacterial overgrowth (SIBO), in which bacteria usually limited to the colon move upward into the small intestine and hamper digestion. Once these bacteria settle nicely in their new home, they begin breaking down carbohydrates through a process called fermentation, which produces excessive amounts of hydrogen and methane gas—the build-up of gas results in upper abdominal bloating and various other symptoms such as pain and nausea.

Hormonal Imbalance

We discussed in the previous chapter how high levels of cortisol could disrupt sleep. Rising levels of cortisol can also cause bloating. Moreover, abnormal levels of the female sex hormones estrogen and progesterone can also cause you to balloon right after having a meal. This is the reason why some women may experience gas and bloating around the time of their periods or during the early stages of menopause when they are going through hormonal changes. The gut microbiome is highly sensitive to changes in hormonal levels (Wheaton, n.d.).

Food Intolerance

The inability to digest certain foods can cause bloating. For example, lactose and gluten intolerant individuals usually experience bloating, abdominal discomfort, and diarrhea after consuming milk or grain-based products. In many cases, dysbiosis can trigger food sensitivities, which causes bloating.

A change in the microbial composition can impact the concentration of different bacterial metabolites. The absence of certain metabolites can disrupt normal systems in the gut, impairing our ability to break down various foods. The rise of bad bacteria can also alter the markers present on food particles called antigens and trick the immune system into producing an immune response such as inflammation (Caminero et al., 2019). Due to dysbiosis, you may experience an allergic reaction to foods that never caused discomfort before.

POPPING THE BUBBLE

One of my favorite books growing up was Roald Dahl's whimsical novel *Charlie and the Chocolate Factory.* At one point in the story, a character named Violet eats a magical bubble gum and balloons into a giant round ball. *"Prick her with a pin,"* one of the other characters suggests as everyone tries to think of ways to bring her to her original size.

Bloating might make you swell to twice your size, but there is a magical pin that you can use to squeeze yourself back to normal. And don't worry, pricking yourself with it won't hurt you in the least bit because the pin I'm talking about isn't a pin at all—it's fiber. The key to deflating your puffed-up body lies in the greens on your plate. Plant foods are rich in fiber, the magic ingredient that can eliminate bloating and gas once and for all.

Make sure you're keeping up in the Workbook. There are really helpful activities related to this chapter

10

ALLERGIC TO THINGS? WE CAN FIX IT THROUGH YOUR GUT

What happens when the world is your oyster, and you are allergic to shellfish?

—Neil Leckman

Sniffle. Cough. Sneeze.

And repeat.

If that's what keeps you indoors during spring when pollen's in the air, then there's a good chance that gut microbes are to blame. Allergies are our body's response to substances that our immune system considers "harmful." These seemingly harmless substances, such as pollen that activate our body's defense system, are called allergens. Let's look at what allergies are and how an imbalance in the gut microbiome could be a contributing factor.

ALLERGIC REACTION

When an allergen enters your body, your immune system reacts by producing antibodies (IgE). This sets off a chain of events leading to an allergic reaction. Antibodies are like commandos deployed by the immune system to hunt down the enemy and mark it for destruction. Once they track down the foreign substance that managed to slip inside, they direct the release of histamine.

In the previous chapters, we briefly discussed the immune system and the role of histamine (the "tough guy"). Let's take a closer look at the intricate system designed to ward off diseases and how a slight malfunction could make you clutch a ball of tissues to your nose when someone brings you flowers.

The Wondrous World Of The Immune System

In Chapter 2, we learned that the immune system behaves like a security checkpoint and adaptive immunity helps us recognize past intruders. Let's try to further our understanding of this complex system and how it could sometimes work against us.

The immune system comprises a network of cells and organs called the lymphoid organs (spleen, thymus, tonsils). These organs are where the white blood cells called lymphocytes are produced. The lymphocytes travel around the body fighting off viruses and bacteria and kicking out allergens through the blood vessels and lymphatic vessels. This network of channels throughout the body carries lymphocytes to the lymphoid organs and bloodstream.

The Search And Kill Operation

Let's meet the commandos unleashed by our immune system to trace intruders. Antibodies are Y-shaped proteins that bind to foreign objects called antigens. An antigen can be any molecule that could be a part of a virus or bacteria. For example, the coronavirus (SARS-CoV-2) has spikes protruding from its outer coat that some antibodies bind to and recognize.

Antibodies bind to antigens using the V-shaped arms on top, while the bottom half, or the stalk, remains attached to immune cells. Once they've apprehended the intruder, they signal the immune system to bring out the executioner to finish the job. Antibodies are also known as immunoglobulins (Ig) and consist of five types: IgG, IgM, IgA, IgD, and IgE. All these immunoglobulins differ from each other slightly in appearance and function, with only IgE being in charge of launching an allergic response (Ghose, 2020).

When antibodies detect an antigen, they send chemical signals to the "mast cells" present in our skin, nose, gut, lungs, and mouth. This signal directs the mast cells to release histamine, which travels toward the allergen. Histamine increases blood flow toward the area, causing inflammation and activating other immune system components to step in and fix the damage.

When they've completed the initial tasks on their agenda, histamines dock at specific locations in the body known as "receptors." So if the allergen entered your body through the nose (pollen, dust, pet dander), then histamines could cause the thin nasal walls to produce more mucus. So you might get a runny or stuffy nose and start sneezing. The excessive amount of mucus generated to eliminate the allergen may trickle down your throat and make you cough, while the inflammation may give you a headache and red, itchy eyes.

Even though symptoms caused by histamines can cause considerable discomfort, it's important to keep in mind that they're a part of our body's defense mechanism to eliminate allergens (Fowler, 2020).

Types Of Allergies

A wide range of substances can evoke an allergic reaction. Some of these include

- Pollen

- Dust mites

- Molds

- Animal dander

- Latex

- Food allergies (milk, shellfish, peanuts, soy, wheat, egg, and tree nuts)

Symptoms Of An Allergic Reaction

Allergic diseases include problems such as eczema, asthma, hay fever, hives, and food allergies. Symptoms of an allergic reaction may range from mild to severe. Common signs of an allergic response based on different affected sites include

Upper Respiratory Tract

- Wheezing

- Coughing

- Sneezing

- Runny nose

- Watery eyes

Skin

- Itching

- Rashes

- Hives

The Digestive Tract

- Bloating

- Nausea

- Constipation

- Diarrhea

- Vomiting

The Nervous System
- Headaches

Anaphylaxis

While the symptoms of most allergic reactions cause mild to moderate discomfort, some allergens can cause a serious, life-threatening reaction called anaphylaxis or anaphylactic shock. The response can last from a minute to an hour after coming in contact with the allergen.

Anaphylaxis involves the swelling of body tissues and a sudden drop in blood flow. The affected individual might feel their throat closing up. Itching, rashes, and hives might appear on most body parts. Other symptoms include:

- Tightness in the throat as the tongue and throat swell up.

- Difficulty breathing

- Feeling warm

- Dizziness

- Headache

- Stomach cramps

- Nausea or vomiting

- Diarrhea

- Feeling light-headed and fainting

- Feeling anxious

- Chest tightness

- Abnormal heart rate (too fast or too slow)

WHY SCIENTISTS BELIEVE GUT BACTERIA ARE TO BLAME

A few years ago, a bite of an egg would make my whole body break out in painful hives. Medicine such as penicillin made my immune system go crazy, and I could not endure having cats or dogs anywhere near me. Like so many others, I accepted my allergies as a part of my life. I had to learn to deal with it because there was no way I could get rid of it.

But everything changed when I came across Cathryn Nagler's research at the University of Chicago. Cathryn suffered severe food allergies growing up and knew first-hand how they could affect life quality. She made a shocking discovery while studying arthritic mice. The immune cells in these mice attacked the collagen proteins in their joints, resulting in severe arthritis.

Nagler and her team realized they could jump-start the disease by injecting the mice with collagen. However, when collagen was administered through a tube snaking down into their stomachs, it helped the mice get better! The discovery baffled scientists.

In 2004, Nagler and her team published a report showing that peanuts cause anaphylaxis only in mice with defective TLR4 receptors. When a significant portion of the microbial population in the gut was wiped out with antibiotics, even mice with normal TLR4 receptors developed food allergies (Landhuis, 2020).

Decades later, the concept of oral immunotherapy emerged, treating food allergies by administering small doses of allergens. This approach has gained widespread popularity, especially given the approval granted by the US Food and Drug Administration in January 2020 for daily capsules to treat peanut allergy (Landhuis, 2020).

Still, oral immunotherapy has a few drawbacks. Daily consumption of food that could potentially kill is stress-inducing for some patients. Moreover, it doesn't work the same for everyone and does nothing to treat underlying issues. After all, the goal isn't for patients to tolerate a mere speck of peanut flour but to be able to eat a handful of peanuts safely.

So, Nagler and her team started looking for easier and more durable ways to treat food allergies. They turned their attention to the gut this time. They singled out dysbiosis as the root cause of allergic reactions. They made significant headway last year when they managed to suppress a severe allergic response in allergy-prone mice by introducing gut microorganisms from non-allergic human babies.

Another scientific breakthrough happened in March 2020 when researchers detected an abundance of antibodies against peanut allergens in the gut of allergic patients. The discovery confirmed the GI tract as the hotspot for food allergies. Further research identified toll-like receptors (TLR4) as the linchpin of the problem.

Based on previous research, scientists assumed that perhaps the trillions of microbes swarming our gut suppress immune responses to food particles by activating the TLR4 receptor. Perhaps changes in the microbiome's composition altered the suppression, leading to a rise in allergies. TLR4 receptors are responsible for the detection of foreign compounds (antigens) and initiate an immune response in return. In the absence of certain microbes, these receptors begin recognizing food particles as a threat and launch a full-fledged attack against the offending compounds.

In the end, allergies appear as a result of our immune system's response to foriegn objects. Gut microbes bind to the TLR4 receptor keeping it busy, so it doesn't initiate an immune response toward non-foriegn objects. Dysbiosis might cause the TLR4 receptor to malfunction. Fixing our gut microbiome can help reduce or eliminate allergic reactions. The studies above show that the gut microbiome lies at the center of problems such as food allergies, which means strengthening our home team is our best shot (Harvard T.H. Chan School of Public Health, n.d.).

PART 3

Let's Fix This
With Plants

11

PLANTS TO THE RESCUE!

Nothing will benefit human health and increase the chances for survival of life on Earth as much as the evolution to a vegetarian diet.

—Albert Einstein
World-renowned theoretical physicist, best known for developing the theory of relativity

We've witnessed the horrors unleashed in the gut by harmful microbes when they manage to outnumber the good bacteria. We've endured the devastating effects of having these malevolent microorganisms running amok in our gut long enough—it's time to settle the score by bringing out the big guns. They're the mean, green killing machines. They're the fresh fruits and vegetables lying abandoned at your local grocery store while you hog the frozen foods section.

So, what makes green leafy vegetables and vibrant, juicy fruits a miracle cure for poor gut health? It's because they are loaded with a magic ingredient that can help wipe out the bad bacteria teeming in your gut and boost healthy microbes. You'll have no trouble figuring this one out if you've been paying attention so far. The magical cure-all ingredient is fiber!

HEAL YOUR GUT WITH PLANTS

Imagine a large round plate with a big red apple next to a few slices of melon and a banana. Crisp, green florets of broccoli lie on the side along with a handful of whole grain pasta. Grilled cubes of tofu, spinach, beans, peas, and a few almonds fill up the rest of the plate. Notice the diverse, bright, colorful foods on your plate: this is what a plant-based diet looks like.

Vegetables, fruits, nuts, whole grains, and legumes are the staples of a plant-based diet. However, some people may choose not to go full vegan or vegetarian. Or, they may choose to slowly phase meat and dairy out of their diet. If meat or dairy products remain alongside your otherwise plant-based diet, try to ensure that you eat larger portions of foods from plant sources.

Plant-Based Diet And Nutrition

Plant-based diets are known to support health, decrease risks of developing cardiac problems, high blood pressure, and diabetes, and increase longevity. They fill us up with essential elements such as protein, carbohydrates, vitamins, fats, and minerals. They also contain copious amounts of phytonutrients (plant chemicals that offer a plethora of health benefits) and—the super element—fiber.

A vast body of research suggests that eating plant-based products can help reset the balance in the gut microbiome. The results are surprisingly quick: a single meal can significantly alter the number and type of bacteria in your gut. A regular plant-based diet can produce long-term benefits by drastically changing the gut microbiome.

The nutrients we consume from food can be grouped into two categories: macro and micronutrients. Macronutrients are required in large quantities to provide us with energy, such as carbohydrates, proteins, and fats. Micronutrients are required in small quantities, such as vitamins and minerals. Let's look at the nutritional advantages of plant-based foods.

Carbohydrates

Carbohydrates make up a huge chunk of our diet. Plant-based foods usually contain high carbohydrate content. *What? That can't be good!* Fitness gurus and the latest fad diets will have you believe carbs are responsible for your weight loss woes; however, these important macronutrients have been wrongly vilified.

Nothing will benefit
human health and
increase the chances
for survival of life
on Earth as much as
the evolution to a
vegetarian diet.

Carbohydrates contain a wide variety of foods that have different effects on our health, weight, and satiety. They are primarily divided into three main groups:

1. **Simple carbohydrates**

   These carbohydrates exist in their most basic form and are referred to as sugars. Examples of foods rich in simple carbohydrates include processed foods such as cakes, candies, and sodas. Fruits and vegetables are also some natural sources of sugar.

2. **Complex, low-fiber carbohydrates**

   They consist of a number of simple sugars that are strung together. They are also known as starches. Our body breaks down long starch molecules into sugar to provide energy. Foods in this category include bread, pasta, cereal, and some vegetables such as peas, potatoes, and corn.

3. **Complex, high-fiber carbohydrates**

   They also consist of a long chain of molecules resembling beads on a string. However, unlike starches, our body cannot break them down into smaller units. We need the help of gut microbes to digest plant fibers and release nutrients. Foods containing high fiber include fruits, vegetables, seeds, beans, whole grains, legumes, and nuts.

Since simple carbohydrates are already present in their most basic form, our body doesn't have to break them down further through the action of enzymes. They are readily absorbed in the small intestine and fermented by the bacteria in the colon. We briefly discussed fermentation in chapter 9 and how it can lead to the build-up of gas if harmful bacteria in the gut exceeds the number of beneficial microbes.

The high fiber content of plant-based diets serves as fodder for beneficial bacteria such as Bifidobacterium, Eubacterium, Ruminococcus, and Lactobacillus. Remember the heroic short-chain fatty acids or SCFAs we met in chapter 4? Fiber is crucial for SCFA production, which plays a key role in metabolism, minimizing inflammation, and preventing gastrointestinal disease. SCFAs also provide energy for colonocytes, strengthen the epithelial barrier, and change intestinal pH, inhibiting the growth of harmful microorganisms.

Proteins

Protein is found in a wide selection of plant products such as vegetables, nuts, seeds, soybean, and grains. Soybean products are an excellent source of protein in particular as these products contain high concentrations of fiber, potassium, magnesium, and folate. Switching to a plant-based diet can reduce our dependence on meat as our primary source of protein.

Excessive meat consumption can produce Trimethylamine (TMA), which is eventually converted to trimethylamine N-oxide (TMAO) by gut microbes. Red meat, shellfish, poultry, and fish contain abundant Trimethylamine-containing compounds such as L-carnitine, choline, and betaine. Some evidence suggests a link between elevated levels of TMAO and the risk of developing cardiovascular diseases (Guo et al., 2020).

Fats

Fats aid the absorption of "fat-soluble" vitamins such as vitamin A, E, K, and carotenoids. They are composed of long chains of fatty acids essential for various biological functions such as reducing inflammation, regulating cholesterol, and maintaining a regular heartbeat. Fats are packed with energy, so overconsumption causes weight gain.

Eliminating fats from our diet completely could lead to a shortfall of fat-soluble vitamins. Opting for healthy fats instead of unhealthy ones ensures we get a steady supply of essential fatty acids and vitamins while avoiding the risks associated with high-fat consumption. Fats can be divided into three groups:

1. Saturated fats

2. Trans Fats

3. Unsaturated fats

Unhealthy fats consist of saturated fats and trans fats. Animal food sources such as meat, dairy, fried, and prepackaged foods are jam-packed with saturated fats. These fats are unhealthy for us because they increase "bad" cholesterol or low-density lipoproteins(LDL). Eating lots of foods that contain saturated fats can cause LDL to pile up on the walls of blood vessels. This build-up is known as plaque.

The constriction of blood vessels due to plaque accumulation can block blood flowing toward the heart, causing angina, heart attack, or stroke. In contrast, "good" cholesterol consists of high-density lipoproteins (HDL), which absorb cholesterol, transporting it to the liver, where it is flushed out of our system (Center for Disease Control, 2020).

Lastly, trans fats are liquid oils that turn into solid fats after undergoing hydrogenation. Trans Fats are excessively troublesome because they increase LDL while decreasing HDL. Processed foods, cookies, cakes, pies, and fried foods are some foods that are bursting with trans fats.

Researchers observed a marked increase in Firmicute and Mollicute populations in the gut of mice when they were fed a high fat and high sugar diet. Dwindling numbers of *Bacillus bifidus,* lactic acid bacteria, and *Enterococcus* were also observed, along with a noticeable reduction in microbial diversity in the gut (Zhang & Yang, 2016).

Plant-based sources of unsaturated fats include avocados, tofu, flaxseed, walnuts and olives. Swapping saturated fats with unsaturated fats leads to more microbial diversity in the gut, and increases the number of beneficial microbes such as *Bifidobacterium bifidum*, *Bacteroides*, and *Prevotella* because these bacteria feed on fibers (Carver, 2021). The combined action of these microbes staves off disease-causing bacteria, brings down inflammation, supplies nutrients, and helps in weight loss.

Phytochemicals

Phytochemicals carry out various essential tasks in plants. For example, one group of phytochemicals called polyphenols contains anthocyanins, which give flowers, fruits and vegetables their vibrant colors. Plant reproduction hinges on these bright pigments because they attract pollinators.

Multiple studies show that polyphenols can help manage blood pressure, keep blood vessels healthy, promote good circulation, reduce chronic inflammation and keep blood sugar levels in check. Some beneficial phytochemicals include flavonoids found in blueberries and cranberries, which support the immune system, regulate metabolism and exhibit prebiotic and antibacterial effects.

Carotenoids found in spinach and carrots can help dial down inflammation. Polyphenols present in honey, peppers, black currants, raspberry, green tea, cinnamon, and peppermint inhibit the growth of *Helicobacter pylori,* promoting Lactobacillus strains instead. Consuming more flavonoids enhances *Bifidobacterium, Lactobacillus,* and *Enterococcus* populations in the gut while decreasing *Clostridium* and *Bacteroides* (Yin et al., 2019).

WHAT SHOULD YOUR PLATE LOOK LIKE

Here's what you should put on your plate when you start following a plant-based diet (Harvard TH Chan School of Public Health, n.d.).

Fruits And Vegetables: ½ Of The Plate

Most of your meals should consist of fruits and vegetables. So, fill half your plate with colorful fruits and leafy green vegetables. And, although nothing beats them when it comes to taste, try to avoid potatoes, which can have an adverse effect on your blood sugar.

Whole Grains: ¼ Of The Plate

One-fourth of your plate should consist of whole grains like barley, wheat berries, oats, brown rice, whole wheat, quinoa, and whole-wheat pasta. This is because whole grains and their products have a low impact on blood sugar and insulin as compared to white rice, white bread, and other refined grains.

Protein: ¼ Of The Plate

The remaining quarter of your plate should consist of protein. Healthy protein sources include beans, nuts, and beans which can be mixed with salads and served with vegetables. Try to avoid red meat and processed meats like sausages and bacon. Tofu, beans, peas, chickpeas, and lentils are great options to fulfill your daily protein requirements if you plan to go entirely meat-free.

Cook Your Food In Healthy Plant Oils

Skip the stick of butter and use moderate amounts of vegetable oils to prepare your food. Olive, canola, corn, peanut, sunflower, and soy are some healthy oil sources. And be wary of the "Low-fat" label on food items. They might contain partially hydrogenated oil or trans fats.

Swap Soda For Tea, Coffee, Or Plain Water

Sugary, fizzy drinks are a big no. Pair your meals with a glass of water. Try to limit milk and dairy products, reducing their intake to one or two daily servings.

 You'll find a plant-based diet plan in Chapter 18, Exercise 1 of the Workbook for the first ten days to help you get started.

Throwing A Feast For The Microbes In Your Gut

What you eat can have an immediate effect on the microbes in your gut. The moment you gobble down that doughnut, the microbes come scampering out their nooks and crannies in the gut to dig into that delicious Boston crème. Armies of disease and inflammation-causing bacteria swell in number the more sugar, unhealthy carbohydrates, and fats you consume, while the good bacteria in your gut remain famished.

Problems arise when the bacteria charged with defending your gut wane in strength and numbers. Your GI tract turns into a battleground as the marauding bacteria tamper with the production of hormones, increase inflammation, and make you vulnerable to diseases. Imagine expecting your troops to fight off a large, approaching army on an empty stomach—it's clear who'd win.

So, when you sit down for your next meal, remember the bacteria in your gut are waiting for what food would appear. Harmful bacteria thrive on sugars, saturated carbohydrates, and fats, while good bacteria prefer fiber, polyphenols, and plant-based proteins. Who would you rather feed? The decision is yours to make.

12

THE MIRACLE WORKERS: FIBER AND PREBIOTICS

Dietary fiber provides a whole slew of health benefits when consumed in adequate amounts. It not only promotes 'regularity,' it also reduces your risk of several chronic diseases and plays a crucial role in successful weight loss.

—Harley Pasternak
Personal trainer, motivational speaker,
TV host, and author

At this stage in the book, you're well aware of the numerous health benefits of dietary fiber. But did you know there are different kinds of fiber? There are tons of benefits of consuming a wide range of fibers, including maintaining a healthy weight and lowering the risk of diabetes, cancer, and cardiac problems.

DIETARY FIBER

Dietary fiber refers to the roughage in our food: the hard stuff we can't digest. Unlike other nutrients such as proteins, fats, or carbohydrates, fiber passes through the digestive system relatively intact because human digestive enzymes can't break it down. Fiber is placed in two groups based on its solubility in water: soluble and insoluble.

Soluble Fiber

This type of fiber soaks up water, making a gel-like substance. It slows down the rate of digestion and helps pare down cholesterol and glucose levels. It is mostly found in plant cells and includes pectins, mucilage, and gums. Oats, peas, beans, citrus fruits, barley, carrots, and apples are common sources of soluble fibers.

Insoluble Fiber

This type of fiber doesn't absorb water. It speeds up the digestive process, which can help relieve constipation. It's found in the structural parts of plant cell walls, including cellulose, lignin, and hemicellulose. Sources of insoluble fiber include whole-wheat flour, nuts, wheat bran, beans, and a wide range of vegetables.

RESISTANT STARCH

While they're not traditionally thought of as fiber, they act in similar ways. Resistant starch is a component of starchy foods that our digestive system can't break down. Several studies suggest that it can improve insulin sensitivity (the responsiveness of your body's cells to insulin), aid in weight loss by increasing satiety, and lower blood sugar levels after meals (*Resistant Starch 101 — Everything You Need to Know*, 2018). It can be found in unprocessed cereals, grains, unripe bananas, lentils, and potatoes.

WHAT HAPPENS WHEN WE DON'T EAT ENOUGH FIBER?

The good microbes in your gut love fiber! However, when they don't get enough of it, they begin munching on the mucus layer lining the gut. The starving bacteria erode the gut lining, making it easy for disease-causing microbes to invade and infect the colon. A team of researchers led by Mahesh Desai at the Luxembourg Institute of Health demonstrated the repercussions of fiber deprivation in the gut of laboratory mice.

The mice, born and raised in a sterile environment, had no gut microbes of their own. These microbe-free mice were transplanted with 14 bacteria commonly found in the human gut and strains of *Escherichia coli*, which can cause diarrhea and inflammation. The rodents were given different diets. The results showed that the mice that received 15 percent fiber from plants and grains had a thicker mucus layer in the gut and succeeded in fighting off infection. When the same mice were given a diet lacking fiber, the gut microbes began attacking the mucus layer.

The researchers also observed changes in the gut microbiome depending on what the furry little animals ate. Some bacteria flourished in the presence of fiber, while others preferred a low or no-fiber diet. Interestingly, the bacteria that thrived in the absence of fiber were capable of breaking down the glycoproteins that made up the mucus layer.

The researchers analyzed the fiber-digesting enzymes produced by the bacteria. They found more than 1600 bacterial enzymes that could break down carbohydrates. Another intriguing feature was the mix of enzymes changed in response to the rodent's diet, with even occasional fiber deprivation increasing the secretion of mucus-degrading enzymes.

Mice that received a low-fiber diet had a thinner mucus layer. While mucus continued to be produced, altered bacterial activity in the gut meant the bacteria ate it faster than it could be replaced. It is almost like an overenthusiastic lumberjack cutting trees faster than new ones have time to grow (Desai et al., 2016).

Now that we have a good idea about why fiber is an essential ingredient in your diet, let's flip open Chapter 12 Exercise 2 in the Workbook open and see if we're eating a sufficient amount. Note down everything you eat in a day and ask yourself if you're providing enough food for your home team. Mark the foods that you could do without and think about healthier alternatives. Your goal is to raise your fiber intake while cutting back on unhealthy foods packed with calories.

FEED THE HOME TEAM; STARVE THE OPPONENTS

Most of us are aware of probiotics but have you heard of prebiotics before? While probiotics are the bacteria living in your gut, prebiotics are the food they eat. Prebiotics consists of soluble and insoluble fiber and resistant starches. Imagine someone who depends on you for nutrition, like a pet. You wouldn't dream of letting them starve. But when it comes to gut microbes—the microorganisms that do so much for us—we don't mind letting them go hungry.

Letting our gut bacteria starve could exact a heavy price from us. Unless we're willing to compromise our health, we better start feeding our little helpers. The chart below lists some of the foods that can help boost beneficial gut microbes. Have a look to check if you're providing enough fuel for healthy bacteria in your diet.

PREBIOTICS AND THEIR BENEFITS

Prebiotic		Nutrient Content	Benefit
Vegetables	Chicory	High fiber (inulin) content	Aids digestion Relieves constipation Antioxidant properties

Prebiotic		Nutrient Content	Benefit
Vegetables	Jerusalem artichokes	Protein Thiamin (Vitamin B) Iron Low glycemic index	Maintains blood sugar levels Improves skin, hair and nails
	Garlic	Vitamin B6 High fiber content (Inulin and fructooligosaccharides)	Antibiotic properties
	Onions, shallots, spring onions	High fiber content (fructans, inulin, fructooligosaccharides) High nutrient content	Aid digestion Antioxidant properties Lower cholesterol
	Leeks	Fructans Vitamin K and C	Antioxidant properties Helps blood clot
	Savoy cabbage	Vitamin A Thiamin Vitamin B6 Vitamin C	Improves skin Heals wounds Protects from premature aging Boosts immunity

Prebiotic		Nutrient Content	Benefit
Legumes	Chickpeas	Protein Vitamin B Iron	Help control blood sugar Aid digestion Lower cholesterol Prevent cancer
	Lentils	High fiber content Folate Potassium Vitamin B1 Iron	Aid digestion Anti-inflammatory Protect the heart Maintain blood pressure Lower cholesterol Maintain blood sugar level
	Red kidney beans	Protein Potassium High fiber content	Prevent colon cancer Improve heart health Control blood sugar levels
	Soy beans	Protein Potassium High fiber content Folic acid Vitamin B	Improve blood circulation Aid digestion Improve heart health Prevent cancer

Prebiotic		Nutrient Content	Benefit
Fruits	Custard apples	Vitamin C	Antioxidant properties
		Iron	Good for brain and heart
		Calcium	Help lower cholesterol
		Vitamin B6	
	Bananas	Vitamin C	Help reduce bloating
		Vitamin B6	Improve heart health
		Magnesium	Aid digestion
		Iron	Antioxidant properties
	Water melons	Vitamin C	Boosts hydration
		Iron	Improves heart health
		Magnesium	Anti-inflammatory
		Potassium	

Prebiotic		Nutrient Content	Benefit
Fruits	Grapefruit	Vitamin A Vitamin C	Manage blood sugar level Help in weight loss Improve brain function Improve heart health
	Raspberries	Polyphenols	Antioxidant properties
Cereal Grains	Bran	Iron Vitamin B6 Magnesium	Lowers cholesterol Helps maintain regular bowel movements
	Barley	Iron Vitamin B6 Magnesium	Immune-boosting function Antioxidant properties
	Oats	Iron Vitamin B6 Magnesium Calcium	Antioxidant and anti-inflammatory properties

Prebiotic		Nutrient Content	Benefit
Nuts and seeds	Almonds	Vitamin E Magnesium Riboflavin Phosphorus	Reduce risk of heart disease
	Pistachio	Manganese Phosphorous Copper Vitamin B6	Maintain blood sugar level Maintain choles-terol Improve heart health
	Flaxseeds	Omega-3-fatty acids Magnesium Iron Calcium Vitamin B6	Lower cholesterol Manage blood pressure Maintain healthy body weight Maintain blood sugar level

Your home team thrives on fibers and prebiotics. To strengthen beneficial gut bacteria we should keep an eye out for insoluble and insoluble fibers as well as resistant starches. Remember that fiber loving microorganisms can quickly turn against you, if they're left feeling hungry for too long. Your gut health will decline as these starving bacteria start attacking the gut lining.

Adding lots of prebiotics to your diet can help keep the number of healthy gut bacteria stable. The foods listed in the table above can work miracles for your gut. So grab a juicy apple or a handful of almonds, as we look at a super-healthy side dish in the next chapter that will add an extra kick of flavor to your meals!

13

FALL IN LOVE WITH FERMENTED FOODS

Fermented foods contain natural probiotics, or healthy bacteria, that can take your health to the next level. Nearly every culture has a version of a fermented food: yogurt, kefir, miso, and fermented vegetables, including sauerkraut, pickles, and kimchi.

—Sara Gottfried M.D.

A few years ago, I came across a strange new food during my globetrotting adventures, called century eggs. The eggs were dark brown and looked transparent—they were the most beautiful thing I'd ever seen, almost too pretty to eat, but I just had to have a bite. They were salty and had a super-soft, creamy texture. Some might describe the egg's taste and smell as pungent, which takes a little getting used to. The most remarkable thing about these eggs was that they were *two months old*!

The Chinese delicacy was discovered 600 years ago during the Ming Dynasty. A homeowner stumbled upon duck eggs lying in a shallow pool of water mixed with lime, which he'd used to construct his house two months ago, and the century eggs were created. The preservation technique prolonged the shelf-life of the eggs significantly.

It's fascinating that fermented foods show up across various cultures around the world. They may have emerged in the limelight as a recent health trend, but they've been a crucial part of our ancestor's diet for centuries. Our ancestors might have been oblivious to the health benefits of fermented foods. They might have been more concerned with food preservation, but managed to boost the nutritional content of foods in the process.

WHAT ARE FERMENTED FOODS?

Fermented foods are created by controlled microbial fermentation. Fermentation is a process that takes place in the absence of oxygen. The microorganisms break down nutrients such as starch and produce gasses, organic acids, and alcohol. The byproducts of this process give fermented foods a delightful texture, taste, aroma, and appearance.

When was the last time you baked bread? There's nothing as divine as the smell and taste of freshly made bread, and it's the perfect example of how fermentation works its magic! The raising agent, yeast, gets to work when you knead that dough and put it aside. Yeast is a fungus that breaks down the sugar in the dough, producing carbon dioxide and alcohol.

When we make bread, we cover the dough and place it somewhere warm. The warmth activates fermentation. The carbon dioxide produced by the yeast gets trapped inside the dough, causing it to rise. Once we pop the dough in the oven, the heat kills the fungus, and the carbon dioxide expands, causing the bread to rise even more. Slice the bread, and you'll find tiny pores inside. These are the tiny pockets where carbon dioxide becomes trapped.

The wonder of fermentation isn't limited to delicious tasting bread. Most whole foods like vegetables, cereals, dairy, and fruits can be fermented. Hundreds of different kinds of fermented foods and beverages offer a wide array of health benefits and a burst of flavor. Some of these include:

- Yogurt
- Kefir
- Kombucha
- Tempeh
- Miso *Yum!*

- Kimchi

- Sauerkraut

BENEFITS OF FERMENTED FOODS

Fermented foods are not just bursting with flavor, they are also the hub of good bacteria or probiotics. Lactobacillus and Bifidobacterium are the most commonly found microbes in fermented foods. These bacteria are known to create a favorable gut environment and strengthen a healthy immune system.

A long list of health benefits is linked to fermented foods, such as the low risk of cardiovascular problems, diabetes, obesity, high blood pressure, and inflammation. They have also been associated with helping maintain a healthy weight, improving brain activity, strengthening bones, and boosting moods.

Moreover, the slew of good bacteria in fermented foods can help decrease LDL cholesterol and improve heart health. It is believed the bioactive peptides, vitamins, and other metabolites produced during fermentation are responsible for the numerous health benefits associated with fermented foods. These compounds help improve blood circulation, nerve function and bolster immunity.

The health benefits of fermented foods depend on the type of microorganisms involved. For example, eating yogurt may decrease your chances of developing type 2 diabetes, while fermented milk, seething with *Lactobacillus helveticus*, may help alleviate muscle soreness (Rapson, 2018).

GUT MICROBES LOVE FERMENTED FOODS, AND SO WILL YOU!

Dig into that kimchi and serve yourself a generous helping of Sauerkraut. The microbes in your gut love fermented food. Adding kimchi, yogurt, and kefir to your diet can enhance microbial diversity in the gut and reduce molecular signs of inflammation.

Researchers at the Stanford School of Medicine set out to put those claims to the test. A clinical trial involving 36 healthy adults explored the benefits of fermented foods. The participants were assigned a high-fiber or fermented food diet for 10 weeks. The two diets affected the gut microbiome and the immune system in remarkably different ways. Consuming yogurt, kimchi, kefir, fermented cottage cheese, fermented vegetables, and kombucha resulted in a more diverse gut microbiome, with larger servings producing stronger effects.

Moreover, the group of people who consumed more fermented foods observed a marked decrease in inflammation. Blood samples revealed reduced levels of 19 inflammatory proteins, including interleukin 6, which has been associated with illnesses such as rheumatoid arthritis, type 3 diabetes, and chronic stress.

On the other hand, blood samples of participants who were given high-fiber diets showed no decrease in the level of inflammatory proteins. Microbial diversity in the gut of these participants also remained stable. The results baffled scientists, who expected to find beneficial effects similar to fermented foods. The data indicated that jacking up fiber intake alone for a short time did not result in a noticeable increase in microbial diversity.

The study, published in *Cell* online on July 12, shows that adding fermented foods to a high-fiber diet is the best method to increase the population of healthy microbes in the gut and lower inflammation. While diets based on high-fiber foods have been linked to several health advantages and lower mortality rates, the addition of fermented foods brings the benefits up a notch. Fermented foods help maintain healthy body weight and decrease the risk of serious diseases such as diabetes, cancer, and cardiovascular problems (Weaver, 2021).

Interestingly, the research findings showed that people with greater microbial diversity in the gut showed a significant decrease in inflammation after eating a high-fiber diet. In contrast, the group that started off with low diversity in the gut microbiome showed an increase in inflammation while eating more fiber.

The researchers believed this could be because the people with a less diverse microbiome lack the microbes that could break down the fiber they ate. Large amounts of undigested fibers were found in the stool samples of these individuals. This confirmed that these people lacked the microbial populations required to digest high-fiber foods. Their gut microbiome needed time to adapt to the new diet. This could explain why some people react poorly to high-fiber diets, initially experiencing bloating and other gastrointestinal discomforts (O'Connor, 2021).

Fermented foods have been around for centuries. They're a dietary staple in several cultures across different parts of the world. People have long known and relied on the process of fermentation to create cheese and bread, preserve vegetables and meats, boost flavor and enhance textures of various foods. It is only now that we've discovered the tons of benefits that these delicious foods have to offer. So next time you sit down to eat, leave some room on your plate for a serving of kimchi or have a sip or two of kombucha. The bacteria in your gut love it, and so will you!

14

KNOW YOUR FRIENDS AND MARK YOUR ENEMIES!

The human body has been designed to resist an infinite number of changes and attacks brought about by its environment. The secret of good health lies in successful adjustment to changing stresses on the body.

—Harry J. Johnson

A few years ago, I traveled to New Zealand and went about exploring the North Island in a rented four-wheel drive. After spending a relaxing day at Hot Water Beach and taking in the breathtaking beauty of Cathedral Cove, I started heading toward the Coromandel coast. The sun dipped below the horizon, painting the sky with different hues of red and orange as my car rattled down the path.

I wanted to avoid traveling at night, so I decided to take "the road less traveled" and cut through the peninsula rather than following the looping coastal route. After a while, the road shrank from two lanes to one, eventually changing into a steep, serpentine dirt track barely wide enough to fit one vehicle. I climbed up the winding path at a snail's pace for an hour with my heart in my throat, terrified that another vehicle might appear in the opposite direction.

Just when I was starting to lose my nerves, the road widened into a large field and I could see hundreds of pigs roaming about! I later discovered that I had stumbled upon a popular tourist attraction on the island: Stu's Pig Farm.

In today's fast-paced life, we're always trying to cut corners and resorting to quick fixes. When a problem looms ahead, it's natural to look for solutions. However, our busy schedules might force us to find faster and easier ways to solve our problems. Short-cuts may help us achieve our goals quickly, but they usually ignore the underlying issues, which means the problem keeps resurfacing. And, more often than not, they might land us in even bigger problems.

THE THREE S'S: SUGAR, SLEEP, AND STRESS

Have you heard of the three sisters? They're called sugar, sleep, and stress. They go hand in hand in destroying your gut health.

Ever since my teenage years, my default strategy for dealing with heartbreak or setbacks has included spending the afternoon gobbling down spoonfuls of ice cream and napping for five hours straight. As Stephen King put it in his book, Doctor Sleep, "Sugar solves lots of problems, that's what I think." The same goes for sleep. Stress triggers you to load up on sugar, curl up on the bed and doze off. It's the perfect combination to chase the blues and help you get back up on your feet. It's the quick fix we all find ourselves gravitating toward at one time or another; however, the more I learned about gut health, the more I realized that my coping strategy for stress had to change. Sleeping and eating a bucketful of ice cream might seem like an excellent pick-me-up at the moment, but it could do more harm than good in the long run.

Here's why you need to roll back your sugar intake and make sure you get the right amount of sleep at night.

WHAT DOES SUGAR DO TO YOUR BODY?

On average, Americans consume 77 grams of sugar every day, a number significantly higher than the recommended daily amount of 25 to 35 grams. For decades, the devastating effects of sugar on human health have been an open secret. It's common knowledge in the scientific community that sugar can disrupt metabolism and insulin responses, which cause a number of downstream effects.

What researchers didn't know was that too much sugar could lead to IBD. We discussed IBDs like Crohn's disease and ulcerative colitis in chapter 4. These dreadful diseases affect almost 3.5 million people worldwide, crippling everyday life through symptoms such as diarrhea, fatigue, weight loss, and abdominal pain.

To discover the mechanism through which sugar influences IBD, researchers observed the effect of different sugars such as glucose, fructose, and sucrose on inflammatory responses and gut microbes in mice.

Researchers administered 90 percent water solutions to a group of mice followed by 10 percent fructose, glucose, or sucrose for a week. The dose was carefully calibrated to match common sodas' 15 percent sugar content. The mice were then given another sugary sweet drink consisting of 2.5 percent dextran sulfate sodium (DSS), a chemical used to induce colitis (colon inflammation).

Meanwhile, another group of mice sipped on high sugar solutions for one to five weeks, followed by a dose of DSS. Both groups were compared to a bunch of healthy mice that did not receive the sugary treats. After these experiments, the researchers went a step further to analyze the effect of sugar on the gut microbiome by transplanting the gut microbes of mice that gulped down sugars into healthy mice.

The results showed that mice on the high-sugar diet suffered from severe colon inflammation, intense diarrhea, and drastic weight loss. Inflammation causing gut microbes saw an exponential rise in numbers in these mice, exacerbating colitis. While short-term intake of heaps full of sugar did not cause severe acute inflammation in mice with healthy guts, it did cause a sharp decline in the population of beneficial gut bacteria, affecting digestive and metabolic processes.

One species of bacteria that particularly loved feasting on the excessive amounts of sugar sent to the gut was *Akkermansia muciniphila*. Emboldened by the massive piles of sugar coming its way, this little scoundrel starts degrading the mucus lining in the gut and leads to colon inflammation.

BUT, WAIT! WHY CAN'T YOU STOP CRAVING SUGAR?

The more you think about scaling back on those delicious cupcakes, the more you want to eat them! So, what's really going on? Why can't you just stop craving sugar?

Driven by the urge to survive, the bad bacteria in your gut will try every trick in the book to make sure you keep feeding them. And if you don't, then they'd be just as happy to eat you!

The microbes in your gut have varying appetites: yeasts love sugar, Bacteroidetes munch on fats, Prevotella gobble up carbs, and Bifidobacteria snack on fibers. And what happens when the food runs out? They try different methods to signal the waiter to bring more. Here's how these wily gut microbes can influence your food preferences:

1. They produce toxins that alter your mood, making you feel miserable, so you'd reach out for more sugary foods.

2. They change your taste buds!

3. They increase the number of opioid and cannabinoid receptors.

4. They alter the production of neurotransmitters such as dopamine and serotonin, affecting our mood. So every time you pop a candy or brownie in your mouth, you get a hit of dopamine. In other words, they reward you for eating more sugar.

The gut microbes use the stick and carrot approach to ensure a steady supply of their favorite foods, but just because they resort to these sneaky tactics doesn't mean you can't break the cycle (Anderson et al., 2019).

SAYONARA SUGAR!

The evidence above underscores the nasty effects of consuming too much sugar. With the above research in mind, quitting sugar should be a piece of cake, right? Here's where things get tricky. Over the past few decades, noting the addictive nature of sugar, manufacturers discovered sneaky ways of adding it to foods where you'd least suspect to find it. Whether or not you've had them recently, I'm sure you know about chicken nuggets and ketchup, right? Well, those crunchy little chunks of meat are loaded with—you guessed it—sugar!

The reality is that you'd be hard-pressed to find processed foods that don't contain sugar. A survey published in *The Lancet* in 2015 found that 68 percent of all packaged foods and beverages in the US contained "caloric sweeteners" or, in other words, sugar (Popkins & Hawkes, 2016).

So, what can you do to reduce the amount of sugar you consume? Here are some suggestions:

- **Get cooking:** The more you opt for homemade foods, the higher your chances are of avoiding sugar-rich processed foods.

- **Avoid sugared foods:** Steer clear of foods like salad dressings, breakfast cereal, and pasta sauce, which contain mountains of sugar.

- **Drink plain water:** Clear out those bottles of juice, cans of soda, and other sweetened beverages from your fridge.

- **Go organic:** The more you eat foods close to their natural state, the healthier you'll feel.

In light of a vast body of research, plant-based foods have the most to offer regarding nutrition and health (Tuso, 2013). While it is near impossible to completely eliminate sugar in our diet since it is an important source of energy and a crucial component of metabolism, we can stop excessive consumption of artificially sweetened foods and beverages.

So, don't hold yourself back from eating your own birthday cake or indulging in a chocolate glazed donut once in a blue moon, but do keep track of how much sugar you're consuming daily and opt for healthier options.

BEFRIEND THE SANDMAN: THE IMPORTANCE OF SLEEP

If you've been pulling frequent all-nighters due to work or staying up binge-watching your favorite shows; it's time to start following a consistent sleeping schedule. Sleep deprivation opens the door to a number of health problems. Not clocking in enough hours of sleep at night means you'll most likely feel on edge all day.

In chapter 8, we learned about the gut clock and how the bacteria in your gut can keep you awake. It's no secret that sleep is crucial for our overall health. A good night's sleep influences your energy levels during the day, helps biological systems function properly, improves immunity, and strengthens the heart, brain, and digestive system.

Sleep and gut health are closely intertwined. Digestive health can determine how many hours of sleep you get at night, and feeling well-rested can impact the function of the digestive system. Our bodies crave a consistent and predictable routine, meaning if we go to bed and wake up at the same time each day, we're more likely to have no trouble falling asleep.

Here are some ways that sleep deprivation can affect gut health:

1. Lack of sleep leads to more stress, which in turn affects the gut microbiome. We discussed in the previous chapters how the rise of the stress hormone, cortisol, can increase intestinal permeability, leading to a condition called leaky gut. Not only does that upset the balance in the gut microbiome, but it also increases the risk of developing

inflammation, suffering from bloating, stomach pains, and food sensitivities.

2. Sleep deprivation makes it difficult to control hunger and may lead to a poor diet. It can increase the production of hormones that generate hunger cues. Moreover, the low energy levels make it more likely that you'd reach for quick energy boosts and consume more processed carbs, trans fats, and sugar.

3. Low production of the sleep hormone, melatonin, has been linked to Gastroesophageal reflux disease (GERD). This is when the stomach acids flow back into the esophagus or the tube that connects the mouth to the stomach.

SOME TIPS TO HELP YOU GET A GOOD NIGHT'S REST

You've sipped chamomile tea and taken calming salt baths, only to lie awake in your bed and stare at the ceiling while the clock ticks past midnight. So, what could make you fall asleep when your mind is buzzing with a million thoughts?

Adults require at least seven or more hours of good-quality sleep every night on a fixed schedule. Here are some tips to make sure you get a restful sleep at night without interruptions:

- Improve your nighttime sleep by making changes to both your day and nighttime routines. Take up an outdoor activity, so you get to spend outdoors in the sunlight.

- Avoid caffeine such as tea, coffee, or soda just before your bedtime.

- Limit naps during the day to twenty minutes or less.

- Drink alcohol in moderation; it can disrupt sleep patterns.

- Avoid having a big meal just before you go to bed.

- Turn off your phone and stay away from electronic devices during bedtime.

- Cut back on smoking. Nicotine found in cigarettes can also make it difficult for you to fall asleep, so try to scale back on those cigarettes or give up the habit altogether if you smoke.

- Follow a consistent bedtime routine and go to bed at the same time every night (Check out Chapter 14, Exercise 4 in the Workbook to create your ideal bedtime routine for maximum sleep).

Greater diversity in the gut microbiome can increase your chances of having a sound sleep. A diverse gut microbiome can impact interleukin-6 production, a cytokine known for its effect on sleep. Microbes that can have a negative impact on sleep include Lachnospiraceae, Blautia, and Corynebacterium (Smith et al., 2019).

HERE'S WHY YOU NEED TO STOP STRESSING OUT

 Just stop stressing and relax!

Has that piece of advice ever worked for anyone? Stress can wreak havoc on the human gut by changing the composition of the microbiome. We discussed in the previous chapters how our brain communicates with our gut through the gut-brain axis. Due to this communication channel between our mind and our gut, our moods can have a huge impact on our digestive system.

Recent research performed on mice shows that social stress can change the composition and behavior of gut microbes. These alterations can severely impact the functioning of the digestive and immune systems. During the experiments, the scientists exposed a group of mice to conflict by pairing them with aggressive mice for ten days. The gut microbiome of these mice was later compared to the gut of mice who did not go through the same ordeal. The most prominent change was observed in two specific types of bacteria: Dehalobacterium and Bilophila. Interestingly, these bacteria species have been linked with autoimmune disorders such as multiple sclerosis (Salvo, 2019).

Genetic analysis of these bacteria showed that their "violent traits" were activated, increasing their number, enhancing movement, and improving signaling between them and the host cells. These bacteria turned into bloodthirsty assassins, prowling through the body and causing infections.

When researchers at the Bar Ilan University in Israel examined the lymph nodes of the stressed mice, they found them packed with disease-causing bacteria and immune T-cells. The results suggested that when the mice were placed in stressful situations, the bacteria in their gut became pathogenic (disease-causing) and started infecting tissues triggering a strong response from the immune system. As the immune cells attack their own tissues, the mice start showing symptoms of autoimmune conditions (Salvo, 2019).

Bringing those stress levels down is essential for your health, but the real question is, *how* do you do it? Knowing the adverse effects of stress on your health is likely to make you more stressed about feeling stressed! If you're wondering how to stop worrying about the little things and the big things in your life, don't sweat because this book has you covered. Here are some tips to ease your worries and help you relax.

FIVE EFFECTIVE STRESS MANAGEMENT STRATEGIES

Living with high levels of stress puts your mental, emotional and physical well-being at risk. You may feel helpless, thinking there's nothing that you can do about it. After all, there's no way to stop the bills from coming in, your work and family responsibilities can't just vanish, and you will never get more hours in a day to get over the mountain of tasks. While it is near impossible to avoid stressful situations, you have control over how you deal with stress, which can make all the difference. Here are five stress management strategies to help you keep anxiety at bay (Robinson et al., 2021).

1. **Identify the Source of Your Stress**

   This might sound easy, and you might have a ready answer. You might think your stress stems from a single factor, such as your job or the piling debt, but you need to probe further and try to get to the root of the problem.

   For example, ask yourself, what is it about your job that makes you feel stressed? Are you always worried about meeting deadlines? Could your procrastination be a contributing factor? Similarly, if you're struggling to pay off mountains of debt, could it be that you're not good at money management?

Keeping a stress journal can help you pinpoint the factors that get you wound up. All you need to do is jot down every time you feel stressed or anxious during the day, what caused it and how you managed to overcome it. You can easily do this in the notes app on your phone. A daily log will allow you to recognize patterns and identify the source of your stress.

2. **Remember the Four A's**

Avoid, alter, adapt, and accept are the four A's that can help you pare down stress. Here's what they mean:

Avoid: Establishing boundaries can help reduce stress levels significantly. Avoid anything that makes you uncomfortable or puts you on edge. Cut toxic people from your life and make self-care a priority

Alter: Sometimes stress is unavoidable. When, despite your best efforts, you find yourself in a distressing situation, focus on what you can do to change it. If you keep getting anxious thoughts, could talking about what's bothering you help you feel better? Are you suffering from burnout, making it difficult to deal with obstacles? Could you take some time off work? Could you try to manage your time more effectively, so you can get more tasks done?

Adapt: The more you think about how horrible something is, the more you feel powerless to change it. Reframe your mindset and look for opportunities in even the bleakest situations. Ask yourself how you could use this moment to improve yourself. Disassociate yourself from the problem and try to look at the big picture. Would you still be worrying about it in a month or a year?

Accept: Accepting things as they are can cause a marked decrease in stress levels. Change your perspective and look for things you feel grateful for, even during setbacks. Let go of things that are out of your control. Forgive yourself for making mistakes, and try looking for the upsides in everything.

3. **Exercise!**

Exercise is an excellent de-stressing activity. The best part is that you don't have to run for miles on the treadmill or spend hours at the gym lifting weights to experience its many benefits. When you exercise, your body releases endorphins, which are hormones that instantly make you feel good.

While you'll reap the most benefits by exercising daily for 30 minutes, even small, seemingly insignificant activities can add up and help you stay fit. Some activities that you can squeeze into your schedule include walking your dog, opting for the stairs instead of the elevator at your workplace, walking or cycling to the grocery store, and playing an activity-based video game. Chapter 17 focuses on effective ways to fit exercise into your jam-packed schedule, so keep on reading to find a solution that works for you!

4. **Practice Better Time Management**

If you're always rushing to meet deadlines, then you might need to brush up on time management skills. Be realistic about the workload that you can manage, and set achievable deadlines.

Prioritize tasks based on their urgency and importance. For example, the most urgent and important tasks should be at the top of your to-do list, such as turning in an assignment. Urgent but not important tasks could include replying to emails, while tasks such as writing 500 words for an essay due next week are important but not urgent. Meanwhile, activities that are neither urgent nor important can wait until you're free.

5. **Adopt a Healthy Lifestyle**

After learning how the bad guys in your gut can tinker with your brain, making you feel horrible, it's clear that adopting a healthier lifestyle can help bring down your stress levels. A healthy plant-based diet ensures your body is well-nourished and prepared to deal with stress. Start your day off with breakfast and keep your energy levels up and your mind sharp by having balanced, nutrient-dense meals throughout the day.

Cut back on sugar and caffeine. The best way to avoid cravings for a can of soda or sugary snacks is to avoid adding the items to your shopping cart at the grocery store. You'll find it much easier to hold yourself back, if your fridge isn't stocked with food that you want to avoid. Also, uninstall food delivery apps from your phone. Try to prepare your own meals as much as possible and reduce the number of times you eat out.

SUPPLEMENTS: YOUR TRUSTED ALLIES

You may feel like you're a lone warrior in your battle against the vicious gut bacteria, but there are some allied forces you can call on to help you secure victory. Dietary supplements are known to boost gut health. They are loaded with vitamins and phytonutrients, which help squash the enemy forces and fortify your defenses. Supplements give an extra kick to your diet by fulfilling all your nutritional needs. The table below lists different food supplements and what they can do for your body (Iliades & Marcellin, 2015).

HEALTH BOOSTING SUPPLEMENTS

Supplements	Natural Sources	Benefits
Vitamin B1 (Thiamine)	Leafy greens vegetables, and beans.	Regulates metabolism. Helps break down carbohydrates into energy.
Vitamin B3 (Niacin)		Aids the breakdown of carbohydrates, alcohol, and fats.
Vitamin B6 (Pyridoxine)		Helps break down proteins.
Vitamin Biotin		Aids the production of cholesterol and the breakdown of fats, carbohydrates, and proteins.

Supplements	Natural Sources	Benefits
Vitamin B12 (Cobalamin)	Leafy greens vegetables, and beans.	It is important for the nervous system. Helps the absorption of folic acid and carbohydrates. Its deficiency can cause anemia.
Vitamin A	Sweet potatoes, kale, carrots, dark green leafy vegetables	Improves vision, reproductive health and strengthens bones. Improves immunity. Its deficiency can lead to Crohn's disease.
Vitamin D	Sunlight, liver, mushrooms, and fortified plant-based milk.	Helps the absorption of calcium, and plays an important role in the nervous, muscular, and immune systems.
Vitamin C	Citrus fruits, berries, broccoli, tomatoes, and peppers.	Strengthens the immune system, prevents colds, improves digestion, and helps the body absorb iron.

Sugar might ease your worries temporarily, but can lead to more problems down the road. The bad gut bacteria have a sweet tooth and will trick you into eating heapfuls of sugary foods. Look out for processed foods, which may contain plenty of sugar in disguise, and swap them with healthier options.

Make lifestyle changes to reduce stress. Establishing firm boundaries, learning better time management, and following a consistent sleep schedule can work wonders for your mental and gut health. Fruits and vegetables are filled with a chockful vitamins crucial for various biological functions. Up ahead we will look at a crucial biological requirement that often gets ignored. Get ready for a big splash!

15

GET
HYDRATED!

Drinking water is essential to a healthy lifestyle.

—Stephen Curry
American professional basketball player

How long can you go without drinking water on a sweltering summer day? Probably not very long. We all know it's important to stay hydrated when the mercury rises, and we're outside. But making sure we're drinking enough water on a daily basis is crucial for our health, regardless of what the thermometer says.

Sometimes, you might get so busy with your work that you may forget to keep track of your water intake. There have been times when I'd get up from my laptop after spending hours working and realize that my throat is parched. It's so easy to forget to maintain your water intake. If it's a particularly hot day, and you end up getting dehydrated, you might experience a headache, feel exhausted, and have trouble concentrating.

Water makes up about 70% of our body weight. It's essential for carrying out a multitude of tasks inside your body, from transporting nutrients to lubricating joints. As such, you might not feel so good if your body's running low on water. Interestingly, the friendly bacteria in your gut feel the same way.

BENEFITS OF WATER

Water has amazing health benefits. It carries out a number of crucial tasks in our body. Here are some of the functions of water in the human body:

1. It transports nutrients and oxygen to the cells.

2. It flushes out problem-causing bacteria and other microbes.

3. It helps digestion.

4. It helps relieve constipation.

5. It regulates blood pressure.

6. It lubricates joints and acts as a cushion.

7. It protects tissues and organs from disease.

8. It regulates body temperature.

9. It helps maintain electrolyte balance.

When your body has enough fluids to execute all of those tasks, it means you're hydrated. Not drinking enough water can put you at risk of dehydration. Exhaustion, dizziness, falling blood pressure, confusion, or dark-colored urine are some signs that you need to drink more water.

HOW DOES WATER IMPACT GUT BACTERIA?

The food you eat has a direct impact on the bacteria in your gut, but did you know that your water choices can influence the gut microbiome in the same way?

The effect of diet on the composition of the gut microbiome has been extensively studied over the past few decades. We know that what you eat can change the number and type of gut microbes within a few hours. Our next meal can also alter different functions in the GI tract and increase or decrease inflammation.

While a healthy plant-based diet is important for improving conditions in the gut microbiome, the quality and quantity of your water intake should also be taken into account. It's easy to ignore how many glasses of water you drink in a day because it is generally not considered an integral part of the human diet. This is one of the reasons that some scientists refer to it as "the forgotten nutrient."

Research involving 2,000 healthy participants hailing from the US and UK demonstrated that water from different sources caused specific microbial populations in the gut to soar. People who drank water from natural sources such as well showed greater microbial diversity compared to people who opted for tap, filtered, or bottled water.

Drinking chlorinated water also harmed beneficial gut bacteria. The quantity of water consumed also played a significant role. People who drank more water had different microbial compositions than those who drank less. For example, the gut of participants who consumed more water showed a low concentration of Campylobacter bacteria, which has been associated with gastrointestinal infections.

The findings of the above studies suggest that a strong link exists between the amount of water we consume and its source on microbial composition in the gut (Prados et al., 2022). So make sure to keep a bottle of sparkling clear water with you while you munch on sauerkraut and fresh green vegetables.

HOW MUCH WATER DO YOU NEED?

So, how many glasses of water do you need to keep things running smoothly inside your body? Generally, about four to six glasses of water a day is enough for most people. However, the amount may vary if you suffer from kidney, liver, heart, or thyroid problems. Some medications such as non-steroidal anti-inflammatory drugs (NSAIDs), antidepressants, and opiate pain medications can also make you retain more water.

Moreover, you may lose or retain more water based on your lifestyle. If you exercise or have a physically demanding job, you may sweat a lot, losing more water than someone who lives a sedentary lifestyle. So there is no one-size-fits-all answer to how much water you should drink in a day. You should adjust the amount according to your lifestyle and health conditions. A general rule of thumb is to drink two to three cups of water every hour or more if you're doing a physically strenuous exercise and sweating heavily.

If keeping track of your water intake seems too much, here's a simple tip to ensure your body is well-hydrated. Make sure to keep a glass of water nearby at every meal. Remember, you can also fulfill your body's water requirements by eating water-rich foods, which include fruits such as watermelon, melons, squash, cantaloupes, and apples, along with crunchy green salads!

16

AVOID UNNECESSARY ANTIBIOTICS

Widespread use of antibiotics promotes the spread of antibiotic resistance. Smart use of antibiotics is the key to controlling its spread.

– A. P. J. Abdul Kalam
The 11th President of India

Alexander Fleming discovered the first antibiotic penicillin in 1928. This life-saving drug helped treat diseases that were deemed incurable, such as gonorrhea, syphilis, meningitis, pneumonia, and endocarditis. The discovery of antibiotics ushered in a new age of medicine, causing a sharp drop in mortality rates worldwide. There is no question that antibiotics marked a turning point in our fight against bacterial diseases by shifting the odds in our favor. A bacterial infection that could make us extremely ill or even kill us could be treated with a single pill.

But, just like anything else, the overuse of these wondrous drugs leads to more problems. Using antibiotics too frequently, especially when they are not the correct form of treatment for a particular disease, only spells trouble in the long run. The Center for Disease Control and Prevention reports that about one-third of antibiotic use in people worldwide is unnecessary and incorrect.

WHAT ARE ANTIBIOTICS?

A sniffle, a cough, or a sore throat—you can make it all go away with an antibiotic. The moment the first symptoms of a cold or flu appear, you yank open the medicine cabinet and pop an antibiotic in your mouth. That should solve the problem, right? And, usually, it does. But here's the catch.

Antibiotics are drugs designed to fight off bacterial infections by either killing the bacteria or stunting their growth and multiplication. They are useless against viral or fungal infections, yet they are mistakenly believed to be the solution to all our health problems. For example, antibiotics are effective against strep throat, but they are not the correct treatment for most sore throats that are mostly caused by viruses. It makes sense, then, that when antibiotics are prescribed for viral infections, they achieve pretty much nothing at all. Your body's immune system has to combat the virus all by itself. When antibiotics are prescribed too often, or if the patient doesn't complete the course, it may give rise to antibiotic-resistant bacteria.

ANTIBIOTIC RESISTANCE

It's alarming that antibiotics that used to be effective against bacterial infections in the past don't work as well anymore. Some drugs have stopped working against bacteria altogether. When this happens, the bacteria that are no longer affected by the antibiotic are termed as antibiotic resistant. Antibiotic resistance is a grave concern for scientists, who fear it could make fighting and eliminating disease much more difficult.

How do bacteria manage to survive such powerful drugs? These single-celled microorganisms multiply at a tremendous speed. As they grow in number, the new generations of bacteria go through genetic variations. Sometimes these changes work in favor of bacteria by making them immune to certain antibiotics. The bacteria that manage to survive an antibiotic treatment multiply, creating more drug-resistant bacteria.

Moreover, some bacteria pass their superpowers to other bacteria as if they're sharing tips amongst each other to help defeat their common enemy. So, while reaching for antibiotics at the first sniffle or sneeze can destroy infection-causing bacteria, it's important to include probiotics in your diet to replenish beneficial bacteria in the gut. *This is a helpful practice.*

ANTIBIOTICS CAN ANNIHILATE YOUR HOME TEAM

The discovery of antibiotics has no doubt been a monumental one for the field of medicine. Just imagine, if it weren't for antibiotics, dental surgery could never have been possible or survivable! However, a heavy dose of antibiotics can unintentionally wipe off beneficial gut bacteria.

An international team of scientists based in Germany examined the impact of 144 commonly used antibiotics on gut health. The study, published in the journal *Nature*, discovered that two classes of antibiotics (tetracyclines and macrolides) caused considerable damage to good bacteria in the gut. This made some people vulnerable to developing gastrointestinal disorders and recurrent infections by *Clostridium difficile* resulting in nausea, stomach pain, and severe diarrhea.

Tetracyclines are classified as broad-spectrum antibiotics, which means they can kill off a wide range of bacteria. As for macrolides, they are used for the treatment of common infections ranging from acne to sexually transmitted diseases. Macrolides can be divided into five types: clarithromycin, azithromycin, fidaxomicin, erythromycin, and telithromycin. These two groups of antibiotics not only thwarted the growth of beneficial bacteria, but also annihilated half of the gut microbial population (Gifford, 2021).

So, what do researchers suggest you do the next time you fall sick? Do they expect you to toughen up and bear the symptoms, hoping that your immune system ultimately prevails against the attacking microbes? Not exactly. It's quite obvious that antibiotic treatment is unavoidable in some circumstances, especially if you're suffering from a disease that could become potentially life-threatening if left untreated. However, you can mitigate the side effects of antibiotics through various methods.

STRENGTHEN YOUR DEFENSES

Health experts such as Professor André Marette from the Department of Medicine at the Heart and Lung Institute, and Scientific director of the Institute of Nutrition and Functional Foods at Laval University, Quebec, Canada and Dr Victor Fulgoni, Senior Vice President of Nutrition Impact, a consulting firm based in Michigan (USA) believe there are other ways of maintaining good bacteria in your gut while you're undergoing antibiotic treatment (Prentice, 2013). Eating a few spoonfuls of yogurt can help replenish beneficial bacterial populations, such as *Lactobacillus acidophilus*. Supplementing your diet with probiotics can also help you maintain steady numbers of certain bacterial strains.

Adding pro and prebiotics to your diet can counter the effects of strong medications by rebuilding and nourishing the gut microbiome. Eating larger portions of plant-based and fermented foods and drinking adequate amounts of water strengthens the bacteria on your home team, improving your immunity and fending off attacking bacteria.

17

GET
MOVING!

Good things come to those who sweat!

—*Anonymous*

Ugh! Another health and fitness book that tells you to exercise, like you don't know that already. What could be more cliché?

I know how you feel. I *hated* exercising, but what I hated more was how every single health expert I met gave me the same advice: *exercise more!* It took me some time to figure out an exercise regimen that was fun and exciting, and didn't make me faint from exhaustion by the end of it. There's no doubt in my mind that you can do the same!

Now, most of us only give exercise a second thought when we're looking to lose weight. Here's something that may come as a surprise: mild to moderate daily exercise can help improve digestive function and alleviate gastrointestinal problems. So, exercising (as much as you might hate it) comes with loads and loads of benefits. It doesn't just help you *look* good, it also makes you *feel* fantastic!

GET UP AND GET MOVING!

By now, you know what you need to do to improve your gut health. But taking probiotics, sipping kombucha, munching on almonds and staying away from sugar and processed foods will fail to help you achieve a healthy gut, if you ignore a major component of the gut health equation.

Here's something to look into: A recent research instructed participants to work out for 30 minutes, three times a week, for a total period of six weeks. The results indicated that certain microbial populations in the gut of the participants increased during this time. The microbes that were positively affected by the exercise included those that could minimize the risk of inflammatory diseases and type 2 diabetes.

If that doesn't make you off that couch and hit the gym, then here's another reason: when you exercise, your body releases endorphins, instantly relieving stress and boosting your mood. However, the trick is to do the right kind of exercise, so you get a nice serving of mood-making hormones with gut-healthy benefits on the side.

Here are some tips to help you reap the maximum benefits of a daily exercise regimen.

1. **Low Intensity, Low Impact Workout Is the Way to Go**

    Start off with low-intensity workouts because high-intensity exercises can be tough on your gut. During an intense workout session, blood flow is directed away from the digestive system and shifted toward your muscles. This means that your digestive system starts slowing down while you're lifting those weights, and sweat's dripping down your face. And while this isn't a cause for alarm at the moment, it can cause some problems once you wrap up your workout session.

    Low-intensity exercise along with a healthy dose of beneficial microbes through a plant-based diet can help relieve constipation by speeding up the digestion system. It can cause more regular bowel movements than spending the day lounging on the couch.

    Exercise at your own pace. Go for dumbbells instead of going for heavy weightlifting or heart-pumping cardio. My go-to exercise routine is going for a thirty-minute walk with my earphones on as I listen to a podcast or music. My advice to you would be to find something you enjoy doing, so it doesn't feel like a chore. Bonus points if you can find something that gets you out in nature, which is an excellent stress reliever.

2. **Don't Rule Out A High-Intensity Workout Altogether**

   As you slowly build up your exercise routine, move on to high-intensity interval training (HIIT). It consists of short periods of intense anaerobic exercise paired with brief recovery periods. It can include activities such as biking, jumping rope, and lifting weights. A HIIT session using a stationary bike would consist of cycling for 30 seconds as fast as you can with high resistance, then allowing yourself a brief period of rest by cycling slowly with low resistance.

   However, it is important to remember that high-intensity workouts that get your heart racing like burpees, box jumps, or squats can cause low levels of inflammation, which is why you should tread with care if you suffer from IBD or IBS. Consuming a plant-based diet that's rich in probiotics can mitigate the effects of this temporary bout of inflammation. As long as you're in good shape and you're eating those leafy greens, continue your HIIT sessions, so get those abs you always wanted along with a healthy gut microbiome.

3. **Listen to Your Gut**

   Let's recap what we learned in the points above: go for a light 30-minute workout in the beginning, and slowly start complementing it with a bit of HIIT. Here's what your workout week should look like if you follow this advice:

try out resistance training twice a week, followed by two days of yoga, and finish off by going for a long hike over the weekend.

You can customize the workout plan above, so you look forward to it instead of dreading it, which will only add more stress to your life, exacerbating symptoms of poor gut health. Pay attention to your gut as you amp up your exercise routine. If your symptoms flare up following an intense workout session doing squats, swap it with a lighter activity the next day like going for a walk. Go for exercises that you enjoy!

REMEMBER, CONSISTENCY IS KEY

You exercise once, and you never gain another pound for the rest of your life.

Who wouldn't want that? Sadly, this is not how exercise works (though we wish it did). The effects of exercise on the gut microbiome last as long as we continue exercising regularly. The same goes for diet; as long as you eat prebiotics, you have healthy bacteria swarming in your gut. But the moment you start stuffing yourself with fried and processed foods, the effects of your plant-based diet begin to fade away. Exercise and diet can work wonders for your gut. Regular exercise helps move waste products through the colon more quickly; it reduces the risk of developing colon cancer, IBD, and diverticulosis. However, to keep experiencing these amazing benefits, we have to make sure we don't give up after the first round on the treadmill. A half-hour low-intensity workout session is enough to drive the bad bacteria away, but it's important that we stick to it daily to see a visible improvement in our overall health.

18

THE PLAN

Never underestimate the power you have to take your life in a new direction.

—Germany Kent
American print and broadcast journalist

Phew! You've done all the heavy lifting and made it to the end. You powered through the complex scientific processes, breezed through complicated names of microorganisms, understood the nexus between the gut microbiome and different biological systems, and made your way out of the rabbit hole!

We started off this journey with a thrilling baseball match between two teams of microbes. Over the next few chapters, we learned more about our gut and the fascinating world of microbes inhabiting our body. We explored the close relationship we share with the microorganisms in our gut and how even a slight upheaval in the gut microbiome ripples through our entire body, affecting virtually every biological function.

We made some shocking discoveries as we learned the effects of our own actions on our gut and how we could be unintentionally arming the opposing team and bleeding our home team. Finally, we were introduced to various methods to shift the odds in our favor and rout the invading group of microbes. Let's round up all the different ways we learned in this book to improve our gut health and beat invading microbes.

1. Eat a predominantly plant-based diet.

2. Pack on those fibers.

3. Eat lots of good fats.

4. Give fermented foods a go.

5. No more sugar to sweeten your day.

6. Kick stress to the curb.

7. Catch up on a good night's sleep.

8. Take daily supplements.

9. Drink loads of water.

10. Cut back on unnecessary antibiotics.

11. Exercise!

A plant-based diet makes up a big chunk of the plan to get your gut health back on track. Interestingly, a survey conducted by Mintel found that 52 percent of adults following a plant-based diet did so because they preferred the taste, while 39 percent cited their health as the motivating factor.

A mountain of research supports the increased health benefits of a plant-based diet and its role in reducing chronic illnesses such as diabetes, cardiovascular disease, and hypertension. A diet rich in vegetables, fruits, and nuts satisfies our basic nutritional needs by providing a steady supply of minerals, fiber, protein, and vitamins. Eating lots of high-fiber foods help bring down cholesterol levels, improve heart health, prevent life-threatening diseases like cancer and help you keep those pounds off.

Despite the many advantages of a plant-based diet, a few risks are associated with it. Cutting out all animal products can cause some nutritional deficiencies. Vegans may find themselves at risk of becoming deficient in vitamin B12, vitamin D, calcium, iron, zinc, and omega-3-fatty acids. However, adding supplements to your diet can help you easily overcome these issues.

Remember that your diet plan should not be too rigid. Spice up your daily meals by trying new foods and avoiding calorie restrictions. You should feel healthy, full, and energized at the end of the day, not deprived of your favorite foods and exhausted. Keep some wiggle room for squeezing in dessert once in a blue moon or a few bites of pizza on your cheat day. Here are some tips for starting out on a plant-based diet.

1. **Slow and Steady Wins the Race**

   If meat currently makes up a large portion of your diet, gradually decrease your meat intake by limiting yourself to eating it only once a day. Going cold turkey will only make it harder for you to control your cravings. You can try going for plant-based foods during the day and only eating meat at dinner. Reframe your mind and start looking at it as a garnish and not the centerpiece of your plate. Eventually, you may choose to scrap it from your daily diet completely.

2. **Swap Animal Proteins With Plant-Based Protein**

   While you try to decrease the amount of meat in your diet, you should make sure you meet your daily protein requirement by eating plenty of plant-based protein sources. Tofu, grains, and legumes are great substitutes for beef and fish.

3. **Healthy Snacks For the Win!**

   Going on a plant-based diet might make you clean out your fridge and get rid of the processed food galore, but it doesn't mean you have to run on an empty stomach all day. When you hear your belly's cries of protest, you don't have to turn the other way. Grab a healthy snack and put those hunger pangs to rest. A small bowl of chunks of fresh fruits, a handful of unsalted almonds, or veggie sticks with hummus dip on the side will make your grumbling tummy sing with your joy and keep harmful gut bacteria in check.

4. **Dig Into Dessert**

   Eating a plant-based diet shouldn't feel like a bummer. There are a number of vegan dessert options to satisfy your sugar cravings. Fresh berries, raisins and other fruits can give your taste buds the punch of sugar they desire without the health risks associated with traditional desserts.

5. **Make Sure You Don't Miss Out on Any Nutrients**

   Make sure to take your supplements after consulting with your doctor, so you receive all the necessary vitamins and minerals. Reaching for foods and drinks that are fortified with vitamin D, B12, and calcium. To meet your daily fatty acid and zinc requirements, make sure to eat sufficient quantities of walnuts, hemp-seed beverages, legumes, and whole grains.

Change can feel frightening sometimes, but if we just hang in there and plow through obstacles, we will eventually emerge stronger on the other side. When I started my journey to improve my gut health, there were several times I wanted to give up and run back to the comfort of my old life. Ditching my old habits and adopting new ones was not easy. I constantly found myself getting pushed out of my comfort zone as I started making tough decisions to secure my mental and physical health.

Sometimes, this meant saying no to a task at work, so I could cut down stress or turning down a late-night meet-up with friends, so I could catch up on my sleep. Sometimes, I had to fight my own urges and cravings to keep my diet on track. I had to drag myself off the bed for my morning walks and force myself to gulp down a glass or two of water every few hours. But in the end, the struggle paid off. I feel better than I've ever felt before, and I want you to experience the same.

The journey you're about to embark on will certainly not be a walk in the park, but it is something you need to do for your health. Changing your lifestyle and switching to a plant-based diet may feel like a bitter pill to swallow, but its massive benefits make all those little daily sacrifices seem like a small price to pay.

The ten-day plant-based diet plan in Workbook Chapter 18, Exercise 1, is designed to help you get started. You'll find some amazing foods that you may not have heard of before. For the recipes, simply type the name of the dish on Google and hit the Search button, then head over to the grocery store to load up on fresh green veggies and bright, colorful fruits.

Best of luck on your new adventure — and happy cooking!

THE TEN-DAY PLANT-BASED DIET PLAN[83]

Meal	Days				
	1	**2**	**3**	**4**	**5**
Break-fast	Tofu scramble with turmeric, pepper, salt, spinach, and whole-grain toast	Whole-wheat tortilla filled with scrambled eggs, peppers, black beans, onions, Monterey jack cheese, and hot sauce or salsa	Pecan granola with fruit salad	Slice of vegan banana bread coated with nut butter	Soy-based yogurt with blueberries and granola
Snack	Roasted edamame	Trail mix made with sunflower seeds, raw nuts, and dried fruit	Whole-grain crackers with hummus	Veggie sticks with hummus	A bowl of mixed fruits and nuts

6	7	8	9	10
Overnight oats with chia seeds and maple syrup	Two slices of whole-wheat toast with almond butter	Omelet with eggs, mushrooms, sautéed red pepper, onion, and spinach	Smoothie with avocado, kale, banana, soy milk, and dates	Chia seed pudding with banana slices and dried coconut flakes
Homemade baked kale chips with hummus	Frozen grapes and a handful of almonds	Guacamole and raw veggies	Roasted chickpeas	Hummus and baby carrots

Meal	Days				
	1	**2**	**3**	**4**	**5**
Lunch	Whole-wheat pasta salad with cherry tomatoes, chickpeas, carrots, red onion, cucumbers, walnuts, olive oil, and balsamic vinegar.	Vegetable and lentil soup and a whole-grain roll	Vegetarian chili with tomato, quinoa, kidney beans, chilis, and black beans	Spinach salad with grilled tofu, cucumbers, chickpeas, tomatoes, walnuts, and a whole-grain roll.	Two slices of toast with avocado and eggs and a side salad

6	7	8	9	10
Arugula salad with quinoa, chopped veggies, black beans, dates, and balsamic vinaigrette	Lettuce wraps with shredded carrots, slices of red pepper, avocado, and chickpeas, and an apple	Spring rolls with peanut dipping sauce and salad with thinly sliced cabbage, edamame, carrots, and sesame oil	Vegetarian pizza topped with mozzarella cheese, tomatoes, broccoli, peppers, onions, and mushrooms	Greek salad with chopped mixed greens, fresh tomato, chickpeas, olives, fresh parsley, feta cheese, extra-virgin olive oil, balsamic vinegar, and whole-wheat pita

Meal	Days				
	1	2	3	4	5
Dinner	Cauliflower pizza crust topped with pizza sauce, roasted red peppers, mozzarella cheese, spinach, and olives	Eggplant Parmesan with zucchini noodles, baked sweet potato and black beans	Grilled vegetable kebabs with grilled tofu, quinoa and spinach salad	Sweet potato tacos with cilantro, black beans, corn tortillas, and brown rice	Black bean burger (use whole-grain bun) with sweet potatoes and roasted broccoli
Dessert	Strawberry lemon oat squares with a spoonful of peanut butter.	Chocolate avocado truffles	Vegan chocolate chip cookies	Citrus olive oil cake	Vegan apple crisp

6	7	8	9	10
Cauliflower, pea, and tofu curry with brown rice and salad	Sweet potato, chickpea, and kale Moroccan stew topped with peanuts with salad	Whole-wheat pasta with cannellini beans and peas and a romaine salad with cherry tomatoes, with a drizzle of olive oil and balsamic vinegar	Zucchini and black bean enchiladas with salsa	Loaded sweet potato with black beans, meatless "beef" crumbles, Greek yogurt, cilantro, and spinach salad
Vegan cheesecake	Sorbet topped with a tropical fruit salad (pineapple, mango, and melon) and shredded coconut	Banana ice cream with nut butter	Fresh strawberries and coconut milk yogurt	Avocado chocolate mousse

IN 90 SECONDS YOU CAN MAKE A HUGE DIFFERENCE

If you feel we've deserved it, please take a moment to leave a review on Amazon.

Your feedback means the world to us. It helps us to improve and it means better learning experiences for all our readers.

We'd be so grateful to you for your review!

REFERENCES

1. Almario, C. V., Ballal, M. L., Chey, W. D., Nordstrom, C., Khanna, D., & Spiegel, B. M.R. (2018, November). Burden of Gastrointestinal Symptoms in the United States: Results of a Nationally Representative Survey of Over 71,000 Americans. *Am J Gastroenterol, 113*(11), 1701 - 1710. 10.1038/s41395-018-0256-8

2. Anderson, S. C., Cryan, J., & Dinan, T. (2019, May 7). *The Shocking Source of Your Cravings*. Psychology Today. Retrieved June 2, 2022, from https://www.psychologytoday.com/us/blog/mood-microbe/201905/the-shocking-source-your-cravings

3. Baylor College of Medicine. (n.d.). *The Human Microbiome Project*. Retrieved March 19, 2022, from https://www.bcm.edu/departments/molecular-virology-and-microbiology/research/human-microbiome-project

4. Bolte, L. A., Vila, A. V., Imhann, F., Collij, V., & Gacesa, R. (2021). Long-term dietary patterns are associated with pro-inflammatory and anti-inflammatory features of the gut microbiome. *Gut, 70*(7), 1287-1298. https://gut.bmj.com/content/70/7/1287.citation-tools

5. Bravo, J. A., Forsythe, P., & Chew, M. V. (2011, September 20). Ingestion of Lactobacillus strain regulates emotional behavior and central GABA receptor expression in a mouse via the vagus nerve. *Proceedings of the National Academy of Sciences of the United States of America, 108*(38), 16050-5. 10.1073/pnas.1102999108

6. Badal, V. D., Vaccariello,, E. D., Murray, E. R., Yu, K. E., Knight, R., Jeste, D. V., & Nguyen, T. T. (2020, December). The Gut Microbiome, Aging, and Longevity: A Systematic Review. *Nutrients, 12*(12), 3759. 10.3390/nu12123759

7.   Begum, J. (2021, October 18). *Irritable Bowel Syndrome (IBS) Symptoms, Causes, Treatments, Medications*. WebMD. Retrieved August 1, 2022, from https://www.webmd.com/ ibs/guide/digestive-diseases-irritable-bowel-syndrome

8.   Blijlevens, N. M.A., & van der Velden, W. J.F.M. (2020). *Mandell, Douglas, and Bennett's Principles and Practice of Infectious Diseases* (Ninth ed.). Elsevier. 10.1016/B978-1-4557-4801-3.00309-X

9.   Caminero, A., Meisel, M., Jabri, B., & Verdu, E. F. (2019, January). Mechanisms by which gut microorganisms influence food sensitivities. *Nature Reviews Gastroenterology & Hepatology, 16*(1), 7 - 18. 10.1038/ s41575-018-0064-z

10.   Carver, C. (2021, April 3). *Boosting fiber intake for 2 weeks alters the microbiome*. Medical News Today. Retrieved May 15, 2022, from https://www.medicalnewstoday. com/articles/short-term-increase-in-fiber-alters-gut-microbiome#Microbiome-composition

11.   Center of Disease Control (CDC). (2020, January 31). *LDL & HDL: Good & Bad Cholesterol | cdc.gov*. Retrieved May 14, 2022, from https://www.cdc.gov/cholesterol/ldl_hdl.htm

12.   Clapp, M., Aurora, N., Herrera, L., Bhatia, M., Wilen, E., & Wakefield, S. (2017, September 15). Gut microbiota's effect on mental health: The gut-brain axis. *Clinics and Practice, 7*(4), 987. 10.4081/cp.2017.987

13.   Chong, P. P., Chin, V. K., Looi, C. Y., Wong, W. F., Madhavan, P., & Yong, V. C. (2019, June 10). The Microbiome and Irritable Bowel Syndrome – A Review on the Pathophysiology, Current Research and Future Therapy. *Frontiers in Microbiology, 10*, 1136. 10.3389/fmicb.2019.01136

14.   *Digestive Disease Continues to Rise Among Americans*. (2021, February 23). GI Alliance. Retrieved March 12, 2022,

from https://gialliance.com/digestive-disease-continues-to-rise-among-americans/

15. Doucleff, M. (2014, April 28). *Got Gas? It Could Mean You've Got Healthy Gut Microbes*. NPR. Retrieved July 30, 2022, from https://www.npr.org/sections/thesalt/2014/04/28/306544406/got-gas-it-could-mean-you-ve-got-healthy-gut-microbes

16. Desai, M. S., Seekatz, A. M., Koropatkin, N. M., & Stappenbeck, T. S. (2016, November 17). A Dietary Fiber-Deprived Gut Microbiota Degrades the Colonic Mucus Barrier and Enhances Pathogen Susceptibility. *Cell, 167*(5), 1339 -1353. https://doi.org/10.1016/j.cell.2016.10.043

17. Diener, C., Qin, S., Zhou, Y., & Patwardhan, S. (2021, September 14). Baseline Gut Metagenomic Functional Gene Signature Associated with Variable Weight Loss Responses following a Healthy Lifestyle Intervention in Humans. *Msystems, 6*(5). https://doi.org/10.1128/mSystems.00964-21

18. *Digestive Disease Continues to Rise Among Americans.* (2021, February 23). GI Alliance. Retrieved March 12, 2022, from https://gialliance.com/digestive-disease-continues-to-rise-among-americans/

19. Distrutti, E., Monaldi, L., Ricci, P., & Fiorucci, S. (2016, February 21). Gut microbiota role in irritable bowel syndrome: New therapeutic strategies. *World Journal of Gastroenterology, 22*(7), 2219–2241. 10.3748/wjg.v22.i7.2219

20. *Ferring and Rebiotix Present Landmark Phase 3 Data Demonstrating Superior Efficacy of Investigational RBX2660 Versus Placebo to Reduce Recurrence of C. difficile Infection - Ferring Global.* (2021, May 21). Ferring Pharmaceuticals. Retrieved March 22, 2022, from https://www.ferring.com/ferring-and-rebiotix-present-landmark-phase-3-data-demonstrating-superior-efficacy-of-

investigational-rbx2660-versus-placebo-to-reduce-recurrence-of-c-difficile-infection/

21. Fields, H. (n.d.). *The Gut: Where Bacteria and Immune System Meet*. Johns Hopkins Medicine. Retrieved April 19, 2022, from https://www.hopkinsmedicine.org/research/advancements-in-research/fundamentals/in-depth/the-gut-where-bacteria-and-immune-system-meet

22. Fowler, P. (2020, June 28). *Histamines: What they do, and how they can overreact*. WebMD. Retrieved May 8, 2022, from https://www.webmd.com/allergies/what-are-histamines

23. Ghose, T. (2020, July 17). *What are antibodies?* Live Science. Retrieved May 8, 2022, from https://www.livescience.com/antibodies.html

24. Gifford, M. (2021, October 21). *Antibiotics Can Kill Healthy Gut Bacteria: Here's What to Eat to Counter That*. Healthline. Retrieved June 6, 2022, from https://www.healthline.com/health-news/antibiotics-can-kill-healthy-gut-bacteria-heres-what-to-eat-to-counter-that

25. Guite, H., & Butler, N. (2021, April 22). *Gut bacteria and inflammation: The role of diet*. Medical News Today. Retrieved April 20, 2022, from https://www.medicalnewstoday.com/articles/how-diet-influences-gut-bacteria-and-inflammation#Conducting-the-study

26. Guo, F., Zhou, J., Li, Z., Yun, Z., & Ouyang, D. (2020). The Association between Trimethylamine N-Oxide and Its Predecessors Choline, L-Carnitine, and Betaine with Coronary Artery Disease and Artery Stenosis. *Cardiology Research and Practice*. 10.1155/2020/5854919

27. Guglielmi, G. (2020, April 10). *The microbiota clock: how gut microbes and circadian rhythms influence health*. MicrobiomePost.com. Retrieved July 4, 2022, from https://

microbiomepost.com/the-microbiota-clock-how-gut-microbes-and-circadian-rhythms-influence-health/

28. Harvard TH Chan School of Public Health. (n.d.). *Healthy Eating Plate*. Retrieved June 8, 2022, from https://www.hsph.harvard.edu/nutritionsource/healthy-eating-plate/

29. Hawrelak, J. A., Myers, S. P. (2004). The Causes of Intestinal Dysbiosis: A Review. *Alternative Medicine Review, 9*(2), 180 - 193. http://www.anaturalhealingcenter.com/documents/Thorne/articles/intestinal_dysbiosis9-2.pdf

30. Hjorth, M. F., Roager, H. M., Larsen, T. M., & Poulsen, S. K. (2018, March). Pre-treatment microbial Prevotella-to-Bacteroides ratio, determines body fat loss success during a 6-month randomized controlled diet intervention. *International Journal of Obstetrics, 42*(3), 580 - 583. 10.1038/ijo.2017.220

31. Harvard T.H. Chan School of Public Health. (n.d.). *The Microbiome*. Harvard T. H. Chan. Retrieved August 1, 2022, from https://www.hsph.harvard.edu/nutritionsource/microbiome/

32. *How Skin Relates to Gut Health*. (n.d.). CLEAR SKY DERMATOLOGY. Retrieved July 30, 2022, from https://clearskydermatology.com/how-skin-relates-to-gut-health/

33. Huang, T.-T., Lai,, J.-B., & Xu, Y. (2019, February 19). Current Understanding of Gut Microbiota in Mood Disorders: An Update of Human Studies. *Frontiers in Genetics, 10*, 98. 10.3389/fgene.2019.00098

34. *Irritable Bowel Syndrome: IBS, Symptoms, Causes, Treatment*. (2020, September 24). Cleveland Clinic. Retrieved August 1, 2022, from https://my.clevelandclinic.org/health/diseases/4342-irritable-bowel-syndrome-ibs

35. Iliades, C., & Marcellin, L. (2015, June 25). *4 Essential Vitamins for Digestive Health*. Everyday Health. Retrieved June 4, 2022, from https://www.everydayhealth.com/

digestive-health/essential-vitamins-for-digestive-health.
aspx

36. International Foundation for Gastrointestinal Disorders.
     (n.d.). *Facts About IBS*. About IBS.

37. Ipsos. (2021, January 18). *45% of people globally are
     currently trying to lose weight*. Retrieved April 23, 2022,
     from https://www.ipsos.com/en/global-weight-and-actions

38. Jain, U., Ver Heul, A. M., Xiong, S., & Gregory, M. H. (2021,
     March 12). Debaryomyces is enriched in Crohn's disease
     intestinal tissue and impairs healing in mice. *Science*,
     371(6534), 1154-1159. 10.1126/science.abd0919

39. Kordahi, M. C., Stanaway, I. B., Avril, M., Grady, W. M.,
     Ko, C. W., & DePaolo, R. W. (2021, October 13). Genomic
     and functional characterization of a mucosal symbiont
     involved in early-stage colorectal cancer. *Cell Host and
     Microbe*, *29*(10), 11589 - 1598. https://doi.org/10.1016/j.
     chom.2021.08.013

40. Landhuis, E. (2020, May 23). *Gut Microbes May Be Key to
     Solving Food Allergies*. Scientific American. Retrieved May
     13, 2022, from https://www.scientificamerican.com/article/
     gut-microbes-may-be-key-to-solving-food-allergies/

41. Lawler, M., & Kennedy, K. (2020, January 9). *Plant-Based
     Diet: Food List and 14-Day Sample Menu*. Everyday Health.
     Retrieved June 8, 2022, from https://www.everydayhealth.
     com/diet-nutrition/plant-based-diet-food-list-sample-
     menu/

42. Martin, A. M., Sun, E. W., Rogers, G. B., & Keating, D. J.
     (2019). The Influence of the Gut Microbiome on Host
     Metabolism Through the Regulation of Gut Hormone
     Release. *Frontiers in Physiology*, *10*. https://doi.org/10.3389/
     fphys.2019.00428

43. McNamara, D. (2021, September 17). *Gut Microbiome Could
     Make Weight Loss Easier for Some*. WebMD. Retrieved

April 27, 2022, from https://www.webmd.com/diet/obesity/news/20210917/gut-microbiome-weight-loss

44. *The Microbiome, Stress Hormones, & Gut Function.* (n.d.). The Institute for Functional Medicine. Retrieved May 2, 2022, from https://www.ifm.org/news-insights/gut-stress-changes-gut-function/

45. The Human Microbiome Project Consortium. (2012, June 13). Structure, function and diversity of the healthy human microbiome. *Nature, 486,* 207–214. https://doi.org/10.1038/nature11234

46. Morowitz, M. J., Carlisle, E., & Alverdy, J. C. (2011, August). Contributions of Intestinal Bacteria to Nutrition and Metabolism in the Critically Ill. *Surgical Clinics of North America, 91*(4), 771–785. 10.1016/j.suc.2011.05.001

47. Mueller, N. T., Zhang, M., Juraschek, S. P., Miller, E. R., & Appel, L. J. (2020, March 1). Effects of high-fiber diets enriched with carbohydrate, protein, or unsaturated fat on circulating short chain fatty acids: results from the OmniHeart randomized trial. *American Journal of Clinical Nutrition, 111*(3), 545-554. 10.1093/ajcn/nqz322.

48. National Institutes of Health, U.S. Department of Health and Human Services. (2009). *Opportunities and Challenges in Digestive Diseases Research: Recommendations of the National Commission on Digestive Diseases.* NIH Publisher. https://www.niddk.nih.gov/about-niddk/strategic-plans-reports/opportunities-challenges-digestive-diseases-research-recommendations-national-commission

49. O'Connor, A. (2021, August 13). *How Fermented Foods May Alter Your Microbiome and Improve Your Health.* The New York Times. Retrieved May 20, 2022, from https://www.nytimes.com/2021/08/13/well/eat/yogurt-kimchi-kombucha-microbiome.html

50. Pahwa, R., Goyal, A., & Jialal, I. (2022). *Chronic Inflammation*. Starpearls Publishing. https://www.ncbi.nlm.nih.gov/books/NBK493173/

51. Pellissier, S., Dantzer, C., Mondillon, L., Trocme, C., & Anne-Sophie. (2014, September 10). Relationship between vagal tone, cortisol, TNF-alpha, epinephrine and negative affects in Crohn's disease and irritable bowel syndrome. *PLoS One, 9*(9). 10.1371/journal.pone.0105328

52. Popkins, B. M., & Hawkes, C. (2016, February 1). Sweetening of the global diet, particularly beverages: patterns, trends, and policy responses. *The Lancet, 4*(2), 174 - 186. https://doi.org/10.1016/S2213-8587(15)00419-2

53. Powell, T. (n.d.). *Energy Balance: Energy In, Energy Out—Yet Not As Simple As It Seems*. Open Oregon Press Books. Retrieved April 26, 2022, from https://openoregon.pressbooks.pub/nutritionscience/chapter/7a-energy-balance-not-simple/

54. Prados, A., Corfas, L., & Clark, A. (2022, January 19). *Is water the forgotten nutrient for your gut microbiota?* Gut Microbiota for Health. Retrieved June 5, 2022, from https://www.gutmicrobiotaforhealth.com/is-water-the-forgotten-nutrient-for-your-gut-microbiota/

55. Rapson, J. (2018, August 20). *What Are Fermented Foods?* Heart Foundation. Retrieved May 20, 2022, from https://www.heartfoundation.org.nz/about-us/news/blogs/fermented-foods-the-latest-trend

56. Ratini, M. (2021, June 2). *Body Composition: Health, Body Fat, and More*. WebMD. Retrieved April 23, 2022, from https://www.webmd.com/fitness-exercise/what-is-body-composition

57. Robinson, L., Smith, M., & Segal, R. (2021). *Stress Management*. HelpGuide.org. Retrieved June 4, 2022,

from https://www.helpguide.org/articles/stress/stress-management.htm

58. Sahar, T., Shalev, A. Y., & Porges, S. W. (2001, April 1). Vagal modulation of responses to mental challenge in posttraumatic stress disorder. *Biological Psychiatry, 49*(7), 637-643. 10.1016/s0006-3223(00)01045-3

59. Salvo, D. D. (2019, May 20). *Could Stress Turn Our Gut Bacteria Against Us? New Research Looks For Answers.* Forbes. Retrieved June 3, 2022, from https://www.forbes.com/sites/daviddisalvo/2019/05/20/could-stress-turn-our-gut-bacteria-against-us-new-research-looks-for-answers/?sh=2fad230247d0

60. Singh, R., Zogg, H., Wei, L., Bartlett, A., Ghoshal, U. C., Rajender, S., & Ro, S. (2021). Gut Microbial Dysbiosis in the Pathogenesis of Gastrointestinal Dysmotility and Metabolic Disorders. *Journal of Neurogastroenterology and Motility, 27*(1), 19-34. https://doi.org/10.5056/jnm20149

61. Smith, R. P., Lyle, S. M., Kapoor, R., & Donnelly, C. P. (2019, October 7). Gut microbiome diversity is associated with sleep physiology in humans. *PLoS One, 14*(10). 10.1371/journal.pone.0222394

62. Sperbe, A. D., Bangdiwala, S. I., Drossman, D. A., Ghoshal, U. C., Simren, M., & Tack, J. (2021, January). Worldwide Prevalence and Burden of Functional Gastrointestinal Disorders, Results of Rome Foundation Global Study. *Gastroenterology, 160*(1), 99 - 114. 10.1053/j.gastro.2020.04.014

63. Stewart, L. (2019, April 30). *The Facts On Inflammatory Bowel Disease And The Gut Microbiome.* Atlas Biomed. Retrieved March 29, 2022, from https://atlasbiomed.com/blog/crohns-ulcerative-colitis-and-the-gut-microbiome/

64. Musso, G., Gambino, R., & Cassader, M. (2010, October). Obesity, Diabetes, and Gut Microbiota. *Diabetes Care, 33*(10). 10.2337/dc10-0556

65. New Life Nutrition. (n.d.). *Is Bad Breath Related to Gut Health?* Retrieved July 30, 2022, from https://www. newlifenutrition.com.au/gut-and-bowel-health/is-bad-breath-related-to-gut-health/

66. O'Connor, A. (2021, March 18). *A Changing Gut Microbiome May Predict How Well You Age (Published 2021).* The New York Times. Retrieved April 7, 2022, from https://www. nytimes.com/2021/03/18/well/eat/microbiome-aging.html

67. Pahwa, R., Goyal, A., & Jialal, I. (2022). *Chronic Inflammation.* StatPearls Publishing. https://www.ncbi.nlm. nih.gov/books/NBK493173/

68. Prentice, A. (2013, October 17). *Experts call for us to eat more yogurt as research reveals its hidden health benefits - FULL COVERAGE.* Yogurt in Nutrition. Retrieved August 1, 2022, from https://www.yogurtinnutrition.com/experts-call-us-eat-yogurt-research-reveals-hidden-health-benefits/

69. *Resistant Starch 101 — Everything You Need to Know.* (2018, July 3). Healthline. Retrieved August 2, 2022, from https://www.healthline.com/nutrition/resistant-starch-101

70. Shariati, A., Fallah, F., Pormohammad, A., Taghipour, A., & Safari, H. (2019, June). The possible role of bacteria, viruses, and parasites in initiation and exacerbation of irritable bowel syndrome. *Journal of Cellular Physiology, 234*(6), 8550 - 8569. https://doi.org/10.1002/jcp.27828

71. Spiller, R. C. (2018, July 11). Hidden Dangers of Antibiotic Use: Increased Gut Permeability Mediated by Increased Pancreatic Proteases Reaching the Colon. *Cell Molecular Gastroenterology Hepatology, 6*(3), 347 - 348. 10.1016/j. jcmgh.2018.06.005

72. Turnbaugh, P. J., Ley, R. E., Hamady, M., Fraser-Liggett, C. M., Knight, R., & Gordon, J. I. (2007, October 17). The Human Microbiome Project. *Nature*, *449*, 804 - 810. https://doi.org/10.1038/nature06244

73. Tuso, P. J. (2013). Nutritional Update for Physicians: Plant-Based Diets. *The Permanent Journal*, *17*(2), 61 - 66. 10.7812/TPP/12-085

74. Venegas, D. P., De la Fuente, M. K., & Landskron, G. (2019, March 11). Short Chain Fatty Acids (SCFAs)-Mediated Gut Epithelial and Immune Regulation and Its Relevance for Inflammatory Bowel Diseases. *Frontiers in Immunology*, *10*, 1664 - 3224. https://doi.org/10.3389/fimmu.2019.00277

75. Wastyk, H. C., Fragiadakis, G. K., Perelman, D., & Dahan, D. (2021, August 5). Gut-microbiota-targeted diets modulate human immune status. *Cell*, *184*(16), 4137-4153. https://doi.org/10.1016/j.cell.2021.06.019

76. Weaver, J. (2021, July 12). *Fermented-food diet increases microbiome diversity, decreases inflammatory proteins, study finds*. Stanford Medicine. Retrieved May 20, 2022, from https://med.stanford.edu/news/all-news/2021/07/fermented-food-diet-increases-microbiome-diversity-lowers-inflammation

77. Wheaton, K. (n.d.). *Bloating - All You Need to Know | Probiotics Learning Lab*. Optibac Probiotics. Retrieved May 5, 2022, from https://www.optibacprobiotics.com/learning-lab/in-depth/gut-health/bloating-all-you-need-to-know

78. WHO. (2021, June 9). *Obesity and overweight*. Retrieved April 23, 2022, from *https://www.who.int/news-room/fact-sheets/detail/obesity-and-overweight*

79. Waclawiková, B., Codutti, A., Alim, K., & Aidy, S. E. (2022, January 3). Gut microbiota-motility interregulation: insights from in vivo, ex vivo and in silico studies. *Gut Microbes*, *14*(1). 10.1080/19490976.2021.1997296

80. Yin, R., Kuo, H.-C., Hudlikar, R., Sargsyan, D., Li, S., & Wang, L. (2019, August 19). Gut microbiota, dietary phytochemicals and benefits to human health. *Current Pharmacology Reports, 5,* 332–344. 10.1007/s40495-019-00196-3

81. Zhang, M., & Yang, X.-J. (2016, October 28). Effects of a high fat diet on intestinal microbiota and gastrointestinal diseases. *World Journal of Gastroenterology, 22*(40), 8905 - 8909. 10.3748/wjg.v22.i40.8905

82. Zhang, Y.-J., Li, S., Gan, R.-Y., Zhou, T., Xu, D.-P., & Li, H.-B. (2015, April 2). Impacts of Gut Bacteria on Human Health and Diseases. *International Journal Molecular Science, 16*(4), 7493–7519. 10.3390/ijms16047493

83. Adapted from everydayhealth.com (Lawler & Kennedy, 2020)

Made in the USA
Las Vegas, NV
02 March 2024

86613261R00115